Usability Testing

A Practitioner's Guide to Evaluating the User Experience

Synthesis Lectures on Human-Centered Informatics

Editor
John M. Carroll, *Penn State University*

Human-Centered Informatics (HCI) is the intersection of the cultural, the social, the cognitive, and the aesthetic with computing and information technology. It encompasses a huge range of issues, theories, technologies, designs, tools, environments, and human experiences in knowledge work, recreation and leisure activity, teaching and learning, and the potpourri of everyday life. The series publishes state-of-the-art syntheses, case studies, and tutorials in key areas. It shares the focus of leading international conferences in HCI.

Usability Testing: A Practitioner's Guide to Evaluating the User Experience
Morten Hertzum

Geographical Design: Spatial Cognition and Geographical Information Science, Second Edition
Stephen C. Hirtle

Human-Computer Interactions in Museums
Eva Hornecker and Luigina Ciolfi

Encounters with HCI Pioneers: A Personal History and Photo Journal
Ben Shneiderman

Social Media and Civic Engagement: History, Theory, and Practice
Scott P. Robertson

The Art of Interaction: What HCI Can Learn from Interactive Art
Ernest Edmonds

Representation, Inclusion, and Innovation: Multidisciplinary Explorations
Clayton Lewis

Research in the Wild
Yvonne Rogers and Paul Marshall

Designing for Gesture and Tangible Interaction
Mary Lou Maher and Lina Lee

Usability Testing: A Practitioner's Guide to Evaluating the User Experience
Morten Hertzum

ISBN: 978-3-031-01099-6 print
ISBN: 978-3-031-02227-2 ebook
ISBN: 978-3-031-00207-6 hardcover

DOI 10.1007/978-3-031-02227-2

A Publication in the Springer series
SYNTHESIS LECTURES ON HUMAN-CENTERED INFORMATICS
Lecture #45
Series Editor: John M. Carroll, Penn State University

Series ISSN 1946-7680 Print 1946-7699 Electronic

Usability Testing

A Practitioner's Guide to Evaluating the User Experience

Morten Hertzum

University of Copenhagen, Copenhagen, Denmark

SYNTHESIS LECTURES ON HUMAN-CENTERED INFORMATICS #45

ABSTRACT

It is all too common for products, such as consumer appliances, information systems, mobile apps, and websites, to cause trouble and frustration. For example, products are often difficult or dull to use, make tasks less flexible or more tedious, shift attention away from important or gratifying activities, and simply fail to deliver expected benefits or experiences. By identifying such trouble and frustration in the lab prior to widespread use, usability tests have proven a valuable method for informing redesign efforts. A usability test consists of having test users exercise a product and think aloud about their experience using it, while an evaluator observes the users and listens in on their thoughts. On this basis, the evaluator identifies usability problems and assesses the user experience. This book describes how to conduct usability tests. After providing context about concepts and testing, the main chapters of the book cover the steps involved in preparing for a usability test, executing the test sessions, and analyzing the test data. Throughout the chapters, concrete guidance is balanced against more complex issues with an impact on the robustness, validity, completeness, impact, and cost of a usability test. The book concludes with an outlook to variations of usability testing and alternatives to it.

KEYWORDS

usability testing, usability evaluation methods, usability, user experience, user testing, thinking aloud, user-centered design, human-computer interaction

Contents

Acknowledgments

I became interested in usability evaluation methods in the late 1990s when usability and user experience were still in the process of establishing themselves as central concerns in product development. This book has grown out of my research on this topic over the many years that have passed since then. Most of this research has been conducted in collaboration with colleagues who have contributed invaluably, and in various ways, to my thinking about usability testing. Without their contributions, I would not have been in a position to write this book. I am particularly indebted to Pia Borlund, Torkil Clemmensen, Erik Frøkjær, Kristin Due Holmegaard, Kasper Hornbæk, Niels Ebbe Jacobsen, Bonnie John, Kristina Bonde Kristoffersen, Jyoti Kumar, Rolf Molich, Qingxin Shi, Xianghong Sun, Hans Sønderstrup-Andersen, and Pradeep Yammiyavar. In addition, I wish to extend my thanks to the many usability professionals who, in spite of their busy schedules, have been prepared to take part in our empirical studies as evaluators.

CHAPTER 1

Introduction

Information technology (IT) has transformed society and continues to do so. Workplaces become increasingly distributed because IT products provide possibilities for communicating and collaborating across distance (Olson and Olson, 2014). Data is heralded as the new oil because IT products provide unprecedented possibilities for supporting decision-making by mining large quantities of data (Javornik et al., 2019). Leisure is increasingly spent indoors engaged in digital media and on-line games (Thulin and Vilhelmson, 2019). Cash is giving way to cards and other forms of digital payment (Arvidsson, 2019), thereby changing the way we experience money. All these changes presuppose well-functioning information systems, mobile apps, websites, and other IT products. To function well, the technical quality of these products must be good but so must their use-related quality. This book is about quality in use, that is, about usability and the user experience.

Products of low usability provide poor user experiences. These products annoy, confuse, delay, frustrate, mislead, stress, and otherwise inconvenience users. Accordingly, they may result in missed deadlines, unintended incidents, erroneous decisions, or failure to complete tasks altogether. Studies suggest that users may be wasting huge amounts of time as a result of frustrating experiences with IT products (Lazar et al., 2006). In addition, a usability problem may have had a decisive influence on the U.S. presidential election in November 2000 (Wand et al., 2001).

To exemplify what a usability problem may look like, Figure 1.1 shows the butterfly ballot used for the U.S. presidential election in Palm Beach, Florida. The butterfly ballot had candidate names on both sides and punch-holes down the middle. You cast your vote by marking the punch-hole that corresponds to your candidate. The usability problem is about establishing this correspondence. Bush voters had to match the first name on the ballot with the first punch-hole; this appears straightforward. Gore voters had to match the second name on the left-hand side of the ballot with the third punch-hole; it appears that they could easily have mismarked their ballots by instead marking the second punch-hole. If they marked the second punch-hole, they voted for Buchanan. Wand et al. (2001) estimate that over 2000 Gore voters may mistakenly have voted for Buchanan. Gore lost the election in Florida with a margin of less than 600 votes to Bush.

The butterfly ballot illustrates that low usability may influence grand-scale decisions but also that designers, occasionally, come up with low-usability solutions. Testing is needed to ensure good usability. A well-established method for this purpose is the usability test (Dumas and Fox, 2012; Lewis, 2012). Other means of usability evaluation have also been devised, including usability inspection methods, which are analytic rather than empirical (see, e.g., Cheng and Mustafa, 2015; Cockton et al., 2012; Nielsen and Mack, 1994). Usability tests and inspections yield feedback to designers about the strengths and weaknesses of their designs. At the outset of projects, design ideas will typically be half-baked and incomplete. Later, and with the feedback from tests, flaws will be weeded out and the design refined. Petroski (1992) argues that the main driver in innovation is to improve on the flaws of existing designs, thereby assigning flaws and the process of finding them a key role in design.

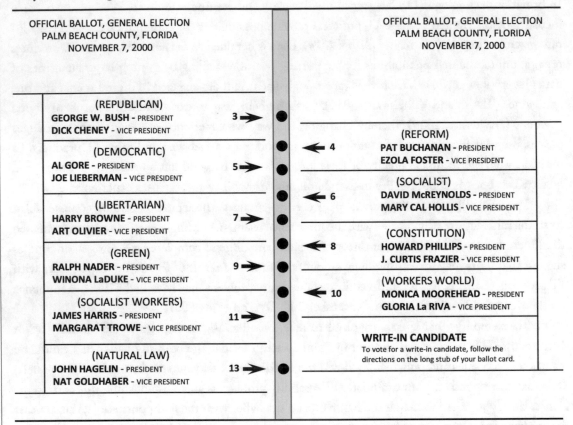

Figure 1.1: The butterfly ballot from the 2000 presidential election in Palm Beach, based on Wand et al. (2001).

1.1   THE BASIC COMPONENTS OF A USABILITY TEST

Usability testing dates back to the early 1970s (Bailey, 1972). An early and influential description of the usability test is the one by Lewis (1982), who called it the "thinking-aloud" method. In essence, a usability test consists of a user who exercises a product while thinking out loud and an evaluator who observes the user and listens in on the user's thoughts, see Figure 1.2. This basic setup allows for numerous variations. At this point, we simply note that a usability test comprises four main components (Clemmensen et al., 2009).

- *Instructions and tasks*: The users interact with the product on the basis of a set of instructions and a set of tasks prepared ahead of the test. The instructions include an explanation of how to think aloud; the tasks prescribe what the users should try to achieve with the product. Thereby, the tasks ensure that the users exercise the product in concrete detail.

- *Verbalization*: While solving the tasks, the users verbalize their thoughts—they think aloud. The verbalizations reveal how the users understand and experience the product. If the users fall silent for longer periods of time, they are prompted to resume verbalization. The users may also be asked to explain why they hesitate, what they expect, and how they assess their experience.

- *Reading the user*: The evaluator, or a group of evaluators, observes the users' interaction with the product and listens in on their thoughts. On this basis, the evaluator analyzes how well the product supports the users in accomplishing the tasks. This analysis results in the identification, description, and reporting of a set of usability problems.

- *Relationship between user and evaluator*: It is the evaluator's responsibility to establish a situation in which the user is able to exercise the product and feels free to make both positive and negative comments. Whether the user is at ease hinges on issues such as instructions, language, and indirect communication cues.

The four components are interrelated and presuppose that the evaluator is familiar with the product and its (intended) uses. These presuppositions mean that a usability test reaches into the preceding analysis and design activities as well as into the subsequent reanalysis and redesign activities. A usability test does not happen in isolation.

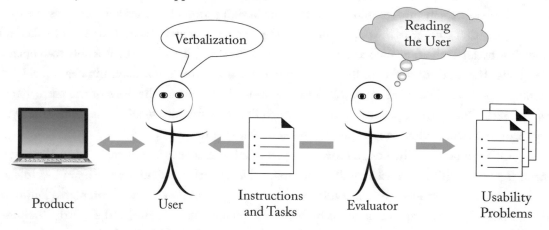

Figure 1.2: The basic components of a usability test, based on Clemmensen et al. (2009).

1.2   THE CONTEXT OF USABILITY TESTS

In the context of this book, usability testing is an activity in the process of product design. Thus, the purpose of usability testing is to inform design. It should, however, be noted that usability tests may also be conducted outside of design processes, for example to inform purchasing decisions or other choices among products that already exist in their final form.

Some models of the design process have evaluation as their pivotal activity. For example, the Wheel model (Hartson and Pyla, 2012) prescribes that the design process should cycle through the activities of analysis, design, implementation, and evaluation, see Figure 1.3. In this model, analysis is about understanding user needs; design is about creating conceptual designs and deciding interaction behavior; implementation is about prototyping; and evaluation is about checking whether the design is on track to meet user needs and requirements.

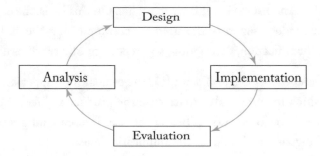

Figure 1.3: The Wheel model of the design process, based on Hartson and Pyla (2012).

The cyclic nature of the Wheel model means that analysis, design, and implementation decisions made during earlier cycles can, and should, be revisited and revised during later cycles, if an evaluation calls them into question. This way, the design process becomes agile and responsive to the insights that emerge as the process unfolds. In principle, any previous decision can be called into question by an evaluation such as a usability test. In practice, it will not be possible to reopen all decisions. The kinds of decisions that can be reopened are, however, not determined a priori by the Wheel model. Rather, it is left for the design team to determine on the basis of the particulars of the project. One of these particulars is cost, which limits—often drastically—the number of cycles that can be performed before the product must be released for use.

Other models of the design process consist of a linear sequence of activities and, thereby, restrict the possibilities for revisiting decisions made during earlier activities, see Figure 1.4. In these so-called waterfall models (Sommerville, 2016), the analysis of user needs is completed before the design begins, the design is completed before the implementation begins, and so forth. The possibilities for evaluation and iteration are, in principle, restricted to the individual phases. The model aims to prescribe that analysis decisions should not be reopened once the process has proceeded to design, and so forth for the subsequent phases. In practice, it may prove necessary to return to a previous phase. While the exact phases differ across instances of the waterfall model, the phases depicted in Figure 1.4 are quite generic. Variants of the model tend to have more, and thus more narrowly scoped, phases rather than fewer phases. Evaluation is not brought to the fore as a separate activity but incorporated in the individual phases. With more narrowly scoped phases, within-phase evaluations become increasingly restricted.

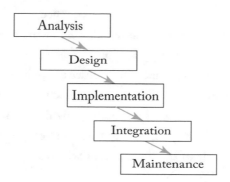

Figure 1.4: The waterfall model of the design process.

Agile methods like the Wheel model are commonplace in, for example, website development. In contrast, the linear, waterfall models are widespread in the development of safety-critical products. Neither the cyclic, nor the linear, models of the design process stipulate a specific number of usability tests. However, the cyclic models assign evaluation a more prominent position and presuppose multiple evaluations over the course of a design project. The waterfall models may not involve any usability testing, they may include some testing, or they may incorporate evaluation in all phases. Usability has become so important to product acceptance and success that usability testing is widespread in design projects (Alves et al., 2014; Gulliksen et al., 2006; Vredenburg et al., 2002), irrespective of whether the projects follow an agile, cyclic, or linear model.

1.3   A SUMMARY OF THE CHAPTERS THAT FOLLOW

The remaining chapters in this book elaborate Figure 1.2. If you are only interested in guidance on how to conduct usability tests, you can skip directly to Chapters 4–7. They are the main chapters of the book. Chapters 2 and 3 provide context about concepts and testing. Chapter 8 concludes the book by providing an outlook to variations of usability testing and alternatives to it.

We start with the concepts of *Usability and User Experience.* Chapter 2 will define what these two concepts mean. That is, it will begin to establish what you are looking for when you conduct usability tests. Multiple definitions exist of usability and user experience because these concepts are employed in diverse practical situations, are part of active research areas, and are influenced by the continuous technological evolution. This book adopts the usability and user experience definitions endorsed by the International Organization for Standardization. To contextualize these definitions we also discuss some of the alternative conceptualizations of the two concepts.

Chapter 3, *Testing: Maxims and Modifications*, will expound what it requires for a usability test to be effective. Initially, these requirements are spelled out in terms of five maxims: robustness, validity, completeness, impact, and low cost. While a usability test ideally achieves all five maxims, they are in practice at odds with each other. As a consequence, usability testing involves a number of tradeoffs through which the maxims are modified. One of the modifications is that robustness tends to come at the cost of validity, thereby forcing a choice of either one or the other. A total of five modifications are discussed to accentuate the realities of applied usability testing. Appreciating the maxims as well as the modifications is pertinent to effective usability testing.

In Chapter 4, *Usability Testing: Step by Step*, the activities involved in conducting a usability test will be laid out. The activities are grouped into three phases: preparations, execution, and analysis. This chapter gives an overview of the three phases, which are covered in detail in the following chapters.

Chapter 5, *Preparations: Designing and Planning the Test*, is about the activities that precede the test sessions. The resulting test will depend on the specific purpose it is to serve and on the time and other resources available for conducting it. The activities in this phase consist of getting to know the domain and prototype, recruiting users, making test tasks, and setting up any equipment. Four key decisions in conducting these activities concern the fidelity of the prototype, the number of users needed, the specificity of the tasks, and the relative focus of the test on effectiveness, efficiency, and satisfaction.

Chapter 6, *Execution: Running the Test Sessions*, will cover the phase from the user arrives until the user has completed the activities involved in taking part in the test. The activities in this phase are welcoming and instructing the users, observing them and listening in on their thoughts, prompting them, taking notes, asking post-task questions, and thanking the users. Four key concerns in conducting these activities are how to make the users feel at ease, how to become sensitized to what they do and say, how and how much to prompt, and how to divide your attention among test-session moderation, on-the-fly analysis, and note-taking.

Chapter 7, *Analysis: Analyzing the Data and Reporting the Findings*, will cover how test data are turned into usability findings. The findings may include both positive and negative usability issues but your primary focus will normally be on the negative issues—the usability problems. This phase consists of analyzing the notes and other test data, rating problem severity, devising redesign proposals, and reporting the test findings. Conducting these activities involves three key concerns: What constitutes a usability problem? How many evaluators are needed? And how to ensure that the test has high impact on the continued development of the product?

Chapter 8, *Variations and Alternatives*, will conclude the book by describing ways in which usability testing can be varied. Seven variations and alternatives are covered: (1) remote usability testing, in which the user and evaluator are at different physical locations; (2) unmoderated usability tests, in which no evaluator is present during the sessions; (3) field usability testing, in which the users exercise the prototype in vivo rather than in a lab; (4) pairwise usability testing, in which thinking aloud is replaced with two users who solve the test tasks together; (5) performance testing, in which thinking aloud is performed retrospectively or not at all; (6) usability specification, in which the identification of usability problems is replaced with the assessment of whether the product meets preset usability targets; and (7) usability inspection, in which no users take part.

This book is intended for students and practitioners who need to learn, or refresh, how to conduct usability tests. The practitioners may be user-experience professionals who have usability work as their primary responsibility or designers who have usability testing as one of their responsibilities along with analysis, design, and implementation. Irrespective of background, usability testing is a nontrivial activity to perform. It is easy to do, but difficult to do well. Doing it well requires a reflective approach that recognizes the complexities, yet stays systematic. This book strives to provide such a reflective approach by balancing concrete, easy-to-follow guidance against more complex, important-to-consider issues. To achieve this balance, the book draws on more than three decades of research on usability evaluation.

CHAPTER 2

Usability and User Experience

Usability tests are a means to evaluate whether a product is usable and how the users experience its use. But what are usability and user experience? In this chapter, we define these two concepts. The definitions are adopted from the International Organization for Standardization and have, thus, gone through a process of proposal, comments, and refinement among experts in the field. In spite of this consensus process, alternative conceptualizations abound. To contextualize the definitions of usability and user experience, we discuss some of these alternative conceptualizations.

2.1   DEFINITIONS

According to Shackel (1984), the first recorded use of the term usability dates back to 1842. Today, the concept has entered everyday language and is ubiquitous in human-computer interaction. The concept of user experience is newer. It emerged in response to a recognition that affect, meaning, value, and the like are important to users' interactions with products but possibly under-recognized by usability, which was seen as focusing mainly on cognition and performance (Hassenzahl and Tractinsky, 2006; Law et al., 2009). Today, the concepts of usability and user experience are often used in tandem. The two concepts overlap but emphasize different aspects of users' interactions with a product. The International Organization for Standardization provides widely used definitions of both concepts (ISO 9241, 2010, p. 3).

- *Usability*: "extent to which a system, product or service can be used by specified users to achieve specified goals with effectiveness, efficiency and satisfaction in a specified context of use."

- *User experience*: "person's perceptions and responses resulting from the use and/or anticipated use of a product, system or service."

The definition of usability contains the four elements commonly used to describe a use situation, see Figure 2.1. By insisting that usability is only defined when these four elements are specified, the definition makes usability an attribute of the use situation, not of the product. Whenever we describe a product as usable, it is a shorthand for saying that a use situation (i.e., a specific configuration of product, users, tasks, and context) works well. It is worth noting the match between the basic components of a usability test (Figure 1.2) and the four elements of the use situation (Figure 2.1). In a usability test, specified users exercise a specified product by solving specified tasks, that is, they work toward specified goals. The one element that may be sacrificed is the context of use, which is largely absent when the usability test is conducted in a lab-like setting away from the users' real work.

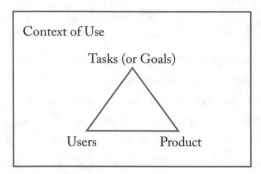

Figure 2.1: The use situation.

The usability definition also stipulates what a usability test must establish. It must establish the extent to which the use situation possesses three qualities (ISO 9241, 2010, pp. 2–3): *effectiveness* (defined as the "accuracy and completeness with which users achieve specified goals"), *efficiency* ("resources expended in relation to the accuracy and completeness with which users achieve goals"), and *satisfaction* ("freedom from discomfort and positive attitudes towards the use of the product").

The definition of user experience makes it a subjective perception. This experience includes "all the users' emotions, beliefs, preferences, perceptions, physical and psychological responses, behaviors and accomplishments that occur before, during and after use" (ISO 9241, 2010, p. 3). Notably, the definition mentions neither tasks/goals, nor context, except in the indirect manner of defining user experience as resulting from use, which presupposes a use situation. The primary focus of the definition is on the user and product. In addition, the definition extends use to include also anticipated use. By explicitly including anticipated use, user experience is also about expectations and the relations between (pre-use) expectations and (in-use) experiences. From an evaluation perspective, the inclusion of anticipated use recognizes the value of testing early on the basis of, for example, mockups and sketches.

2.2   OTHER VIEWS ON USABILITY AND USER EXPERIENCE

There is no shortage of alternative takes on usability and user experiences. Tractinsky (2018) argues that usability is an umbrella concept and, thus, vague and loose. Umbrella concepts are prevalent in diverse and context-sensitive domains that lack a unifying research paradigm. This appears an apt characterization of human-computer interaction (HCI), the research domain that encompasses usability testing. In the absence of a unifying paradigm, concepts tend to denote broad ideas and lack agreed-upon definition. By describing usability as an umbrella concept in spite of the ISO

9241 definition, Tractinsky (2018) emphasizes the presence of competing conceptualizations. He considers this state of affairs inferior to a definitive usability concept, which would define the exact attributes of the concept and provide validated instruments for its measurement. However, a definitive concept also entails the risk of becoming a formal quest for conceptual precision at the expense of practical relevance (Hertzum, 2018).

As an alternative to definitive concepts, Blumer (1954, p. 7) proposes sensitizing concepts, which "suggest directions along which to look." Thus, a genuine understanding of the usability of a product requires a capacity for approaching usability from multiple points of view so that one becomes sensitized to the various elements that impact the use of the product. To this end, Hertzum (2010) presents six images of usability, see Figure 2.2. In spite of a shared essence, these images differ in mindset and perspective. Each image suggests a different direction along which to look and provides only a partial view of usability. It is only by bringing multiple images to bear that you become sensitized to the rich variety of elements that enters into the user experience. The six images of usability are as follows (Hertzum, 2010).

Universal usability: This usability image embraces the challenge of making products for everybody to use. People's abilities, backgrounds, personal styles, technological environments, and so forth are diverse. Yet, all people may need, or want, access to information or some of the other opportunities provided by websites and other products (Stephanidis et al., 2012). Consistently excluding certain groups of people from these opportunities is incompatible with general notions of a fair society. Excluding sizable groups of people from the use of individual products may diminish the feasibility of developing these products. Therefore, it is a compelling goal to design products that are usable for all—a goal quite different from the "specified users" of the ISO 9241 (2010) definition. Universal usability is a grand challenge because it involves that products must be as inclusive as humans are diverse. Universal usability is particularly relevant in relation to the testing of general-purpose products, walk-up-and-use systems, and a variety of web applications, such as e-commerce, e-government, and e-health.

Situational usability: This image corresponds to the ISO 9241 (2010) definition of usability. It is based on the premise that users do not experience products in isolation but as part of a use situation. Consequently, usability must be understood in relation to specified situations with their users, tasks, and wider context of use (Figure 2.1). Simply put, the particulars of the use situation are imperative to whether a product is usable. This situatedness outweighs general usability principles. Draper (1993) considers the situational image of usability pessimistic because it rejects generalization beyond specified use situations. While this largely implies that universal usability is an unattainable goal, it is consistent with basic HCI principles such as "know thy user" (Kim, 2015). Situational usability is directly applicable to the testing of products that are developed with specified use situations in mind, rather than for a market of diverse customers and use situations. Such products include bespoke products, which are commissioned by a customer and custom-built, or configured, for this particular customer's situation.

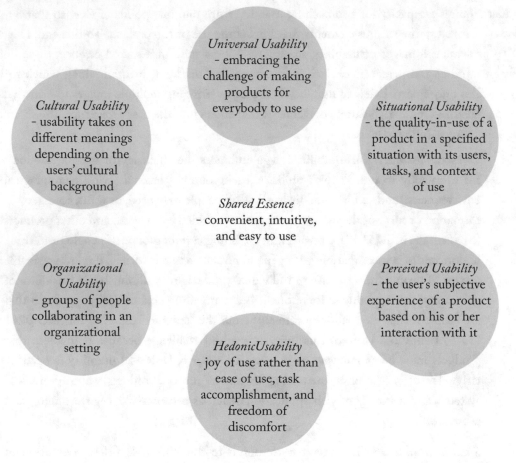

Figure 2.2: The six images of usability, based on Hertzum (2010).

Perceived usability: According to this image, usability concerns the user's subjective experience of a product. Perceived usability is truly user-centered, as opposed to use-centered, because it makes the individual user the final arbiter on usability. This image carries no particular focus on satisfaction but merely a focus on subjective assessments, as opposed to performance measures. People's intention to use a product depends, to a considerable extent, on their perceptions of the usefulness, ease of use, and enjoyment associated with using the product (Hornbæk and Hertzum, 2017). These three perceptions correspond roughly to effectiveness, efficiency, and satisfaction. They demonstrate how perceived usability extends beyond satisfaction and, for example, influences users' intention to use a product, their ways of interacting with a product, and their future purchasing decisions (e.g., Han et al., 2001; Hornbæk and Hertzum, 2017). Perceived usability is especially relevant when evaluating products the use of which is discretionary.

Hedonic usability: This image holds that usability is about joy of use rather than ease of use. Hedonic usability is related to the satisfaction component in the ISO 9241 (2010) definition of usability, but while this component appears biased toward avoiding negative emotions, hedonic usability is all about producing positive emotions. This distinction is important because the qualities that help avoid negative emotions are different from those that produce positive emotions (Helander and Khalid, 2006). Hedonic usability is similar to perceived usability in its focus on subjective experience, but it is distinct from the other images in its exclusive focus on pleasure and emotion. Hedonic usability is particularly relevant to the evaluation of consumer appliances, online games, social media, and other products that involve having a good experience or expressing oneself. In addition, hedonic usability is relevant to e-commerce because the presence of hedonic qualities impacts buying decisions (Jordan, 1998).

Organizational usability: According to this image, usability implies groups of people collaborating in an organizational setting. None of the four previous images have mentioned collaboration or organizations, even though products such as information systems abound in organizations. While a product is expected to provide collective benefit to an organization, there may be individual users who do not benefit. Frequently, some users are tasked with additional work to enter or process information; other users reap the benefits that accrue from this additional work (Grudin, 1994). The uneven distribution of work and benefits means that different user groups may perceive the product quite differently. Elliott and Kling (1997) propose that organizational usability should be assessed at three levels: the user-product match, the organization-product match, and the environment-product match. The second and third levels, in particular, recognize that organizational usability is affected by the ways in which products make some competences obsolete, reroute information, create new roles, and so forth. This image of usability is relevant to the evaluation of products that range from groupware used by organizational subgroups at their own discretion to corporate systems used by all employees on a daily basis.

Cultural usability: This image emphasizes that usability takes on different meanings for users with different cultural backgrounds. Cultural usability can be defined as "the extent to which a computer system, especially in intercultural contexts of use, matches the cultural background of its users, such that it supports their activities effectively, efficiently, and pleasurably" (Hertzum, 2010, p. 584). Many product elements may be culture-dependent, including colors, graphics, language, and layout (Callahan, 2005; Marcus and Gould, 2012). For example, the color red is associated with danger in the U.S. but with happiness in China; in Egypt the color associated with happiness is yellow, which in the U.S. signals cowardice (Thorell and Smith, 1990). In addition to such interface-level differences, people's cultural backgrounds influence their cognitive processes—the way they know the world (Nisbett et al., 2001). These differences in cognitive processes create cross-cultural differences in what constitutes a usable design. Cultural usability is particularly relevant to the evaluation of products for international audiences, including web applications. International audiences may be internal to a single country or organization.

The six images of usability serve to elaborate and contextualize any one definition of usability. Being aware of all six images makes it easier to appreciate the focus and limitations of each of them. While a single usability image will normally dominate in any given test, you should not focus exclusive on one image throughout a development project. Rather, you are advised to enrich your understanding of the usability of the product by, occasionally, applying an alternative usability image to challenge the dominant image. The rationale for this advice is that the usability images are interrelated, but different. They sensitize you to different aspects of the user experience. In choosing an image for a usability test, you should consider the product to be tested and the objective of the test.

CHAPTER 3

Testing: Maxims and Modifications

Effective usability testing is dependent upon a good test method, including good fits between the test and the use context and between the test and the encompassing development process. In this chapter the requirements for effective usability testing are spelled out in terms of five maxims. However, these maxims are at odds with each other. Consequently, applied usability testing involves a number of tradeoffs through which the maxims are modified. Five such modifications are discussed. Appreciating the maxims as well as the modifications is pertinent to being able to conduct effective usability tests.

3.1 FIVE MAXIMS

Ideally, a usability test is robust, valid, complete, high-impact, and low-cost, see Figure 3.1. The three first of these maxims are akin to the general methodological requirements of reliability, validity, and generalizability (Shadish et al., 2002). The two last maxims are about incorporating the usability test in the product development process. Failure to achieve any of the five maxims threatens the quality and usefulness of the test. This is apparent when the maxims are described in more detail (see also, Hertzum, 1999).

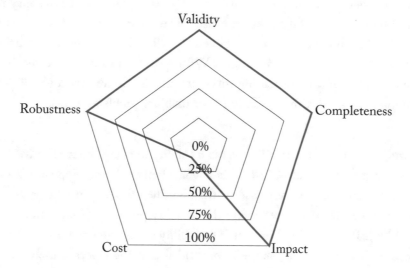

Figure 3.1: Maxims of usability testing.

Robustness: A test method is robust when it produces fairly stable results across a range of variations in the test situation. Such variations may, for example, include the group of user representatives participating in the test as test users, the order in which the test tasks are presented to the users, the evaluator conducting the test, and whether the users think aloud concurrently, retrospectively or not at all. Unless the test method is robust, it cannot be assumed that a rerun of a test will yield essentially the same results. If the results vary considerably from one test of a product to another test of the same product, then the test is not convincing and the results may mislead (Lewis, 2001b). The more robust a usability test is, the more useful its results are.

Validity: A usability test differs from real use situations in that some aspects of the test are not part of real use, just as some aspects of real use are not part of the test. For example, users rarely think aloud during real use and the outcome of tasks rarely has consequences for users during usability tests. The closer the test situation is to real use, the more ecological the test. Ecological gaps between the test situation and real use threaten the validity of the test (Thomas and Kellogg, 1989). A test that lacks validity suffers from two shortcomings. First, the problems that occur during the test may not exist during real use. Second, the problems that hamper real use may not surface during the test. As a result, usability tests are misleading unless their results are valid.

Completeness: A test method that robustly reveals valid usability problems may still reveal only part of the full set of problems. For example, the test tasks may not cover the full functionality of the product or the test users may not represent the full diversity of the user population. An incomplete usability test merely gives a partial picture of the usability of the tested product. With a partial picture it is difficult to assess product quality and prioritize improvement efforts. Conversely, a usability test that is complete, at least with respect to major usability problems, provides direction and a firm footing.

Impact: The impact of a usability test is its ability to bring about effective changes in the tested product. That is, impact is about whether the development team is persuaded to make fixes in response to the identified usability problems and whether these fixes are effective at removing the usability problems (John and Marks, 1997; Law, 2006). The most direct impact of a usability test is in relation to the development team, which may—or may not—be persuaded that the reported usability problems warrant product revisions. However, a usability test may also have an impact on management, marketing, or service by persuading them to reallocate resources, modify selling points, or expand product documentation. Whenever a validly identified problem is left unaddressed, an opportunity to improve the tested product is missed. That is, the effort that went into finding the problem is wasted.

Cost: Usability testing entails expenses for equipment, evaluator competences, compensation to users, and hours for running and analyzing test sessions. In addition to the cost of finding the usability problems, the total cost of a test also includes the cost of addressing the problems found. Several studies aim to justify the cost of usability tests by converting the estimated benefits of performing the tests into cost savings (e.g., Bias and Mayhew, 2005). However, the subjective experience of many developers is that usability work adds expenses, lengthens projects, and fails to prevent that new problems show up when the products are released. As a result, practitioners tend to show a strong preference for low-cost usability tests.

3.2   MODIFICATIONS IN PRACTICE

While the five maxims may sound indispensable, usability tests rarely achieve them in practice—for multiple, good reasons. The ideal depicted in Figure 3.1 masks that practitioners face conditions and tradeoffs that modify the maxims. Appreciating these conditions and tradeoffs is important to understanding usability testing. Specifically, the modifications of the maxims influence what you can conclude from a usability test. In interpreting test results, you should heed the following modifications.

First, *robustness tends to come at the cost of validity*. For example, in-the-lab usability tests provide a controlled environment in which various sources of variability can be kept to a minimum. The controlled environment yields robustness but at the expense of reducing naturally occurring variability, thereby lowering validity. Conversely, in-the-field usability tests are sensitive to the dynamic particulars of real use situations. While this ecological sensitivity bolsters validity, it also implies a lack of control that threatens robustness. That is, a rerun of the test will likely encounter different particulars and, therefore, yield different results. This tradeoff between robustness and validity is not specific to usability tests but common to empirical methods. It has led McGrath (1981, p. 179) to conclude that "all research strategies and methods are seriously flawed; often with their very strengths in regard to one desideratum functioning as serious weaknesses in regard to other, equally important, goals."

Second, *validity is hard to assess*. As a result, it often receives scant attention. For robustness, we can run the test twice and compare the results; the overlap (or lack thereof) is a direct indication of the robustness of the test. For validity, we usually cannot know until much later (e.g., by comparing test results with hotline calls) whether the problems reported from a usability test actually confuse users, slow them down, or otherwise degrade their user experience. The research on the validity of usability evaluation methods mainly targets methods other than usability testing and does it by treating a usability test as the authoritative yardstick against which the other methods are compared (e.g., Bruun et al., 2009; John and Marks, 1997). This approach is flawed because it remains contested under which conditions usability testing is valid (e.g., Hertzum et al., 2009; Olmsted-Hawala et al., 2010).

Third, *completeness may be tradable in formative, as opposed to summative, tests*. Most usability tests are formative. A formative test aims to inform efforts to improve products and will often be part of an iterative design process (Nielsen, 1993). The main goal of a formative test is to provide insights that can feed into the design process and help improve the product. In contrast, a summative test is unrelated to product-improvement efforts. It approaches the product-as-is and aims to assess its usability, for example to determine which of two existing products is preferable. While completeness is pertinent in summative tests, it is less important in formative tests where subsequent design iterations will provide new opportunities for finding any problems missed in the current test. It may be argued that unless you have the resources to fix a problem before the next test, it is inconsequential whether you find it in the current test (Wixon, 2003). But it may also be argued that you misinterpret product status if usability tests are incomplete, especially if they fail to identify high-severity problems.

Fourth, *early tests have higher impact but later tests are more valid and complete*. The impact ratio of a usability test is the number of solved problems divided by the total number of problems found (Sawyer et al., 1996). This simple measure provides a rough indicator of the action taken in response to a usability test. Whiteside et al. (1988) report an impact ratio of 65% for the early, in-house tests of a product and 48% for the subsequent field tests. Hertzum (1999) reports impact ratios of 74%, 73%, and 0% for user tests conducted 5, 8, and 13 months, respectively, into a 14-month development process. The first of these tests was a robust-over-valid usability test conducted in the lab; the last was a valid-over-robust test in the field. In discussing when to evaluate, Buxton (1987) notes that "it is always too early (for rigorous evaluation) until, unfortunately, it's suddenly too late." Thereby, he pinpoints the tradeoff between impact (which points toward testing early) and validity and completeness (which point toward testing late).

Fifth, *it is costly to achieve robustness, validity, and completeness*. There are many threats to robustness, validity, and completeness. The competences, details, and test sizes required to avoid these threats may seem daunting and may lead practitioners to give up on usability testing altogether. To counter this risk, the use of usability evaluation methods must be sufficiently easy, fast, and low-cost to match practitioners' competences, budgets, and time schedules. Otherwise, the methods are not usable. However, ease, quickness, and low cost cannot be achieved for free; they come at the cost of reduced robustness, validity, and completeness. The resulting methods are sometimes referred to as discount methods. Nielsen (1993) advocates that though discount evaluations are inferior to deluxe evaluations, discount evaluations are cost-effective and vastly superior to doing no evaluation work at all. This argument has been very influential, though some have asserted that the methods, and the research into their qualities, may be damaged merchandise (Cockton and Woolrych, 2002; Gray and Salzman, 1998). At the least, the tradeoffs involved in discount methods necessitate that their reduced robustness, validity, and completeness are factored into the interpretation of test results.

The modifications of the maxims mean that applied usability testing involves tradeoffs: You have to think about what it is most important to achieve in each usability test. This clarification should be made in collaboration with the client who commissions the test. Once you have agreed upon what it is most important to achieve, the test should be designed accordingly. And the test results should be interpreted while keeping in mind the tradeoffs intrinsic to this test design.

CHAPTER 4

Usability Testing: Step by Step

The rationale for conducting usability tests is that, in spite of our best efforts, early designs tend to be flawed. Early designs may: (1) match the users' needs or workflows poorly; (2) presume knowledge that the users do not possess; (3) present useful functionality in ways the users do not notice; (4) use confusing terminology; (5) require too many steps to complete a task; (6) include interaction sequences that lead to dead ends; (7) violate standards the users take for granted; (8) impose an inordinate mental workload on users; (9) increase the risk of errors; (10) provide inadequate feedback to lead users to task completion; (11) lack aesthetic qualities; (12) be cumbersome to use; or (13) just fail to surprise and thrill. Usability testing helps identify such usability problems and assists in improving the early designs. In this chapter we presume that the decision to conduct a usability test has been made. Thus, the question is how to perform the test.

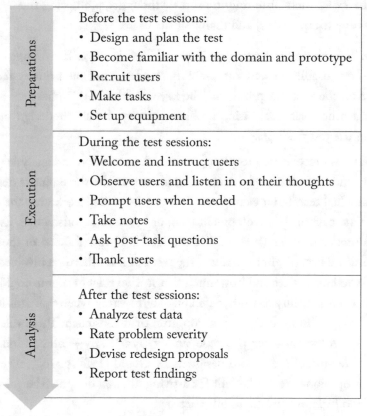

Figure 4.1: The three phases of a usability test.

A usability test can be broken into preparations, execution, and analysis, see Figure 4.1. The preparations are the activities involved in transitioning from the encompassing development project to the usability test. The analysis includes the activities involved in transitioning from the test back to the development project. In between preparations and analysis, the execution of a test is the activities that enter into running the test sessions. That is, the three phases in a usability test are as follows.

Preparations: This phase involves designing and planning the usability test. The resulting test will depend on the specific purpose it is to serve and on the time and other resources available for conducting it. The key activities are familiarizing yourself with the domain and prototype, recruiting users, making test tasks, and setting up any equipment that will be used during the test sessions.

Execution: This phase consists of running the test sessions. A test session starts with the user's arrival and ends when the user has completed the activities involved in taking part in the test. The key activities in this phase are welcoming and instructing the users, observing them, listening in on their thoughts, prompting them, taking notes, asking post-task questions, and thanking the users.

Analysis: This phase turns test data into usability findings. The findings may include both positive usability issues and usability problems, but the primary focus will normally be on the usability problems. The key activities in this phase are analyzing the notes and other test data, rating problem severity, devising redesign proposals, and reporting the test findings.

The preparations precede the execution, whereas the execution and analysis may, partly, run in parallel. The scope and complexity of the activities in each of the three phases depend on the particulars of the individual test. It, for example, influences the activities whether the test is performed by evaluators who are part of the development team or by external consultants. Evaluators who are part of the development team know about the product and project ahead of the test. In contrast, external consultants are brought in to perform the test but not otherwise involved in the project.

It is not easy to know when and how much to test. Two rules of thumb could be that to derive maximum benefit from usability testing you should start testing when you still feel a bit unready to do so and that you are more likely to test too little than too much. These rules of thumb echo Gould et al. (1991), whose third key principle simply says: "Early—and continual—user testing." The following comments, collected from designers by Gould (1988, p. 761), reveal that standards and designers' own opinions are insufficient for arriving at good designs. The comments are informal indicators of too little or too late usability testing.

• "We didn't anticipate *this*."

- "But that is not how I *thought* it worked."

- "What do users *really* want?"

- "I'm too pooped to change it now—it took so long to get here."

- "Why is user testing so late?"

- "I would've tested but…"

- "We are surprised that…"

- "Even simple changes are hard."

- "The help system will take care of this…"

- "A hot-line will take care of this…"

- "It's not broken; that's how it's supposed to work."

If you hear such comments on your project, you know that you have not observed and listened to enough users to be able to design a product that provides a good user experience. Or you have done so too late. Or your usability testing has had too little impact on the product. At the same time, it must be acknowledged that no amount of usability testing provides a guarantee against usability problems. In summary, Table 4.1 provides an overall checklist of issues to consider when deciding to conduct a usability test. The three subsequent chapters contain checklists directed specifically at the preparations, execution, and analysis.

Table 4.1: Checklist – overall issues
☐ A prototype—low-fidelity or high-fidelity—is ready to be tested (otherwise it is still too early for usability testing)
☐ Evaluators—one or several—with the necessary competences have been assigned to the test (otherwise the test results may be contested, left unused, or misleading)
☐ The resources—people, time, and equipment—allocated to the test match its purpose (otherwise revisit Chapter 3 on the maxims and modifications of usability tests)
☐ Users are willing to travel to the lab to participate in the test (otherwise consider remote, unmoderated, or field usability testing, see Sections 8.1–8.3)
☐ A sufficient number of users is available for the test—without depleting the pool of users needed for later tests (otherwise consider a usability inspection, see Section 8.7)
☐ Resources are available for revising the product on the basis of the test results (otherwise it is too late for usability testing)

CHAPTER 5

Preparations: Designing and Planning the Test

A usability test starts with preparations ahead of the test sessions. The basis for the preparations is the embedding development process. This process defines the inputs available for conducting the test and the outputs expected from it. Preparing for a usability test involves five activities, which must be completed before the test sessions can be run.

- Designing and planning the test, including its relative focus on effectiveness, efficiency, and satisfaction (Section 5.1).

- Becoming familiar with the domain and prototype, including issues to do with the fidelity of the prototype (Section 5.2).

- Recruiting users, including the decision about how many users to run (Sections 5.3–5.4).

- Making test tasks, including considerations about their specificity (Section 5.5).

- Setting up any equipment that will be used during the test sessions (Section 5.6).

Table 5.1: Checklist – preparations
☐ The purpose of the test has been specified and the test has been designed in accordance with this purpose
☐ The preparations have been set down in a test plan that, at least, specifies the purpose, task list, user characteristics, and timetable of the test
☐ The evaluator is familiar with the domain or supported by someone with domain knowledge
☐ The evaluator is familiar with the prototype and knows, if it is a low-fidelity prototype, how to simulate its responses to the users' actions
☐ The test users represent the intended user groups and have been recruited in sufficient numbers
☐ Test tasks have been made and they neither use product terms, nor hint at required user actions
☐ For open-ended test tasks: the tasks invite users to bring their real-world experience to bear on the prototype and, thereby, help clarify user needs
☐ For specific test tasks: the tasks are specified in concrete detail and the evaluator knows what needs to be included for a solution to be complete
☐ The equipment for recording the test sessions has been set up and the test location (the lab, company conference room, hotel meeting room, or other space) is ready

Table 5.1 provides a checklist to help determine whether the preparations have been completed and the test can proceed to the execution of the test sessions. None of the checklist items can be bypassed without jeopardizing the test, but resource scarcity may mean that some items are done more thoroughly than others.

5.1   DESIGN AND PLAN THE TEST

Embarking on a usability test involves some level of uncertainty—and may even feel a bit unnerving: Do we know enough about user needs to conduct a test? Is the prototype good enough to enable effective testing? Have we got the design all wrong? However, the absence of such questions would be a bigger problem; it would indicate that you had probably waited too long with testing. Their presence emphasizes the need for planning the test. If the test is conducted early in the development process, you may not yet have a clear sense of the user needs. An early test should help you learn more rather than focus on issues that presume clarity about user needs. If the test is conducted after many design choices have already been made, the test is more likely about refining a design that can no longer be changed fundamentally. It is important to spell out what the test should help clarify and to design it accordingly.

One way to specify what the test should help clarify is to determine its relative focus on effectiveness, efficiency, and satisfaction (Section 2.1). It may be tempting to presume that an effective product is also efficient, an efficient product also satisfying, and a satisfying product also effective. However, studies show that such correlations cannot be presumed to hold (Frøkjær et al., 2000; Hornbæk and Law, 2007). For example, Frøkjær et al. (2000) find that the variation in task completion time (i.e., efficiency) explained a negligible 2% of the variation in the quality of task solutions (i.e., effectiveness). Relatedly, Nielsen and Levy (1994) find that in 25% of the reviewed usability comparisons the users preferred the product with which they were less efficient. That is, effectiveness, efficiency, and satisfaction should be considered largely independent unless domain-specific evidence suggests otherwise. It is risky to conclude anything about, say, the effectiveness of a product from a usability test in which only efficiency and satisfaction data have been collected. Typically, effectiveness will be the major issue in early tests because it relates to whether the product provides the right functionality.

Another way to specify what the test should help clarify is to determine which of the six usability images to apply in the test (see Section 2.2). To evaluate hedonic usability you will design your test in one way, to evaluate organizational usability you will design it in another. Therefore, the focus on one or the other image should be determined during the design and planning of the test, or even earlier. It should not be postponed until the analysis of the test sessions.

Specifying what the test should achieve amounts to determining the objective of the test (the why). This specification shapes the entire test. The design and planning of a usability test also involves specifying what is tested (the product), who the test users are (the user characteristics), how the test sessions are organized (the test design, task list, and test moderation), what data are collected (logging and post-task questions), and when and where the test is conducted (the logistics and equipment). Rubin and Chisnell (2008) advise that the design-and-planning specifications are made manifest in a test plan.

By writing the plan down, rather than holding it in your head, it becomes a blueprint for the test and a key communication device. A written test plan provides a means of stating decisions made and checking off preparations that have been completed. However, the added cost of committing the plan to writing may lead to merely writing parts of it down, such as the task list. The more similar a test is to previously conducted tests, the less risky it is to forego part of the writing. But it is not risk-free. If the test plan is not written down, then it cannot, at least not to the same extent, be negotiated with the client. That is, it cannot be used as a vehicle for ensuring the client's buy-in to the design of the test. Once the client has bought into your test plan, they are more likely to use your test results.

In addition to the task list, you will almost necessarily have to write out a timetable. The timetable specifies when the test activities will be performed and, thereby, how long it will take to conduct the test. Depending on, among other things, the competing commitments of the people involved, the duration of a usability test may range from a few days to several months of calendar time (Dumas and Redish, 1999). The unrelenting pressure of project deadlines and the widespread adoption of agile development methods push the duration of usability tests toward days and weeks rather than months. Based on a survey of 155 usability practitioners, Følstad et al. (2012a) report that the median time spent preparing, executing, and analyzing a usability test is 48 working hours. However, the time spent varies substantially: 25% of the survey respondents spend less than 24 hours and 25% spend more than 80 hours. With progressively fewer hours, your test will be more and more restricted in the number of users you can run and the types of analyses you can make.

The design and planning of a usability test should be led by a user-experience professional. This person brings knowledge about how to conduct usability tests. However, many design-and-planning decisions require input from, and collaboration with, other participants in the development process (Dumas and Redish, 1999). The designers and developers understand the product and what it aims to support users in doing. The technical communicators know the product documentation and which parts of it that need testing. Marketing knows who the prospective users are. The help desk knows about the problems users experience with existing product versions. Management decides the resources allocated to the test.

5.2   BECOME FAMILIAR WITH THE DOMAIN AND PROTOTYPE

Although evaluators are more or less experienced in conducting usability tests, they only conduct their first usability test once. Subsequently, they extend and hone their evaluation skills. Conversely, evaluators may, over time, evaluate products for a range of domains and, therefore, repeatedly face domains in which they have little or no experience. With increasing domain complexity, the evaluators' limited domain knowledge becomes an increasing hurdle to effective usability tests (Chilana et al., 2010; Redish, 2007). If the evaluators are also involved in project activities such as requirements specification and task analysis, they may already be familiar with the domain when they start to prepare the usability test. If not, they may learn about the domain from other project participants who are involved in these activities. Domain knowledge is also available from the prospective users of the product. Talking to people with domain knowledge is a valuable supplement to gleaning it from the task analysis, use cases, and similar project documents.

In simple domains, the evaluators mostly need to apply their existing knowledge to the domain in question. They do not need substantial amounts of new knowledge. Products for simple domains include those that target the general public but also a wide variety of products for smaller, unspecialized target audiences. In complex domains, Chilana et al. (2010) propose forming partnerships with domain experts. Such partnerships are valuable, if not necessary, in testing products targeted specifically at anesthesiologists, baristas, concierges, database administrators, electrical engineers, flight attendants, geoscientists, hair stylists, insurance brokers, journalists, and other specialist domains in which the evaluator lacks knowledge. The domain experts may assist throughout the usability test—from preparations, through execution, to analysis. They may, for example, assist in understanding domain terminology, answering domain-related questions from test users, and prioritizing test findings.

The evaluators also need to familiarize themselves with the prototype if they are not already familiar with it, for example because they have been involved in creating it. They need knowledge of the prototype for the other test preparations, such as for making test tasks. They also need it for activities during the subsequent execution and analysis phases. Prototypes differ in fidelity. These differences influence how the users perceive and react to the prototype. It is important that the fidelity of the prototype matches the purpose of the test. A prototype can be low fidelity or high fidelity (Rudd et al., 1996).

Low-fidelity prototypes demonstrate the general look of the interface. They visualize concepts, depict screen layouts, and illustrate design alternatives. Because they serve communication and evaluation purposes only, they can be made with tools and materials tailored for these purposes. Consequently, low-fidelity prototypes include storyboard presentations, paper mockups, wireframes, and other rapidly constructed, interface-only prototypes. Their limited interaction capabilities and lack of real functionality make them incapable of showing in detail how the product operates.

High-fidelity prototypes enable users to click buttons, enter data, follow links, and interact with the prototype as though it were a real product. They may be developed with dedicated prototyping tools or they may be early versions of the real product. In the former case, they will be discarded after the usability test (just like low-fidelity prototypes). In the latter case, they are made with the tools for developing the real product and intended to evolve gradually into the real product. Their high fidelity makes these prototypes suited for evaluating details in the product design.

During test sessions, the users interact with high-fidelity prototypes like they would interact with the real product—by manipulating the interface, examining the resulting response, and so forth. In contrast, the limited interaction capabilities of low-fidelity prototypes mean that they often do not respond by themselves. When the users indicate that they want to click a button, follow a link, or perform other interface manipulations, then the evaluator steps in and simulates the response of the product. In a paper mockup, the evaluator may, for example, manually replace the paper card that depicts the current screen with that of the screen that matches the user interaction. To be able to simulate the product in a fluent manner, the evaluator must know the prototype thoroughly and devote considerable attention to the simulation task. This task leaves less attention for observing the users' reactions and listening in on their thoughts.

Low-fidelity prototypes may appear primitive—unrealistic for the users, taxing on the evaluator, and too unlike a real product. They have clear limitations, but they also have important strengths, see Table 5.2. Several studies find that usability tests of low-fidelity prototypes identify substantially the same sets of usability problems as tests of high-fidelity prototypes of the same product. The identified problems are similar in number (Sim et al., 2013; Virzi et al., 1996) as well as severity (Catani and Biers, 1998). It appears that the users compensate for the unfinishedness of low-fidelity prototypes by mentally filling in the gap between the prototype and a functional product (Sauer and Sonderegger, 2009). However, other studies find that low-fidelity prototypes lead to other interaction patterns than high-fidelity prototypes and, as a result, to differences in the number and type of usability problems identified (e.g., Derboven et al., 2010; Lim et al., 2006).

Derboven et al. (2010) find that their low-fidelity prototype helped generate design ideas about user interactions, but they also caution that the user interactions attempted on the low-fidelity prototype did not generalize to the high-fidelity prototype. The generation of design ideas is pertinent to usability tests that are conducted early in the development process. Tohidi et al. (2006a) assert that early tests should focus on getting the right design (i.e., on the exploration of design options), while late tests should focus on getting the design right (i.e., on the refinement of a single design). Low-fidelity prototypes are about getting the right design. Contrary to high-fidelity prototypes, they do not give the impression that the product has already almost been finalized. Thereby, a low-fidelity prototype communicates that many design decisions are still to be made and that critical comments and creative ideas are welcome (Snyder, 2003). In addition, the evident un-finishedness of low-fidelity prototypes invites feedback on their overall structure and basic concepts rather than on details such as alignment and colors.

The low cost of developing low-fidelity prototypes makes it affordable to develop several low-fidelity prototypes, each depicting one design alternative. Users are less reluctant to voice criticism when they are presented with prototypes of alternative designs, rather than with only a single prototype (Tohidi et al., 2006a). Their subjective ratings of prototype features are also less prone to inflation. Experiencing multiple alternative designs facilitates the users in thinking about how each individual design might have been different and in calibrating their ratings. The presence of multiple alternative designs makes it less socially stressful to voice criticism because the criticism will often be in terms of preferring one alternative over another, rather than in terms of not liking the only prototype presented in the test.

Table 5.2: The relative effectiveness of low-fidelity and high-fidelity prototypes

	Strengths	Limitations
Low-fidelity prototype	• Fast and cheap to create • Provides substantive user feedback early in the development process • Affords the creation and testing of alternative designs • Communicates the concept well and therefore useful for proof-of-concept testing • Invites creative feedback and design ideas • Avoids the possibly intimidating presence of fancy technology	• Requires that a human facilitator runs the prototype • Gives a limited impression of navigation and flow • Gives no impression of response times • Covers error handling poorly or not at all • Does not demonstrate technical feasibility • Is of limited utility after requirements have been established
High-fidelity prototype	• Can be operated by the users during tests • Conveys navigational scheme • Includes (partial) product functionality • Allows for testing usability in detail • Invites feedback on problems and on poor fit to user practices • Has the look and feel of a real product	• Slower and more expensive to create • Restricted to the refinement of a single design • Inefficient for proof-of-concept designs • Ineffective for requirements gathering • May give a misleading impression of response times

5.3   RECRUIT USERS

Users differ. Some users may have difficulty using a product feature that other users find intuitive or even enjoy. Reasons for such differences include varying levels of experience with similar features in other products, different expectations about how the product works, dissimilar inclinations to explore product features in the face of uncertainty, and differences in the level of attentiveness to labels and other interface elements. Because users approach tasks differently, they may also exercise different parts of the product in trying to solve a test task. Thus, some users experience a feature and, on that basis, find it easy or difficult to use. Other users do not even come across the feature and, hence, cannot say whether it provides a good user experience.

Because users differ, the recruitment of users is crucial to the validity of a usability test. Unfortunately, it cannot be known ahead of a test whether two possible test users will experience the product similarly or differently. Instead, the recruiting of test users must rely on demographics and other factors that can be established ahead of the test. Some products target audiences with specifiable demographics. For example, an app for midwives targets a predominantly female audience with a specific job role and a narrow range of educational backgrounds. For such products, the test users should, if at all possible, have demographics similar to the target audience.

Other products have multiple subgroups of users. Imagine, for example, an electronic health record with information about hospital patients' condition and treatment. This product will be used by physicians, nurses, therapists, hospital pharmacists, medical secretaries, management, and others. Each of these user groups have different roles and responsibilities toward the patients and will, therefore, use the product differently. Because they use the product differently, it is unlikely that they will experience the same usability problems. For example, the problems experienced by a nurse will likely not be the same as those experienced by representatives of the other user groups. In addition, it may be necessary to subdivide the nurses depending on whether they work at, for example, a medical ward, a surgical ward, or an intensive care unit because these groups of nurses have different work tasks, different information needs, and different documentation responsibilities. Consequently, they use different parts of the product—or use the same parts but in different ways.

The subgroups of users may already have been identified and described in the development activities that precede the usability test. If so, this information should be consulted. If not, the user population must be divided into subgroups during the preparations for the usability test. A thorough way of establishing the subgroups of users is the persona method (Marshall et al., 2015; Nielsen, 2019). Alternatively, you may walk through the product and visualize the users of its different parts. For each user group identified, you should indicate their (professional) background, main use of the product, level of experience, and other pieces of information that are deemed relevant. At the end of the walkthrough, you will have produced a matrix characterizing the user groups of the product. In producing this matrix, several overall distinctions should be kept in mind.

- *Average user versus user representative*: The average user is unlikely to exist in practice but may serve as a useful abstraction against which to assess user groups. For example, the user representative in the encompassing development process is more often a product champion or user advocate than an average user (Rasmussen et al., 2011). You are advised to bypass these user representatives in the recruitment of test users.

- *User versus purchaser*: The purchaser is the person who makes the decision to buy the product and make it available to users. In organizational settings, the purchaser will often not be a user himself or herself and will, therefore, know little about the particulars of using the product. You probably would not want to include the purchaser among the test users.

- *Data-entry user versus product-output user*: In organizational settings, some users are often tasked with data entry, while others reap the benefits that accrue from the output generated on the basis of these data (Grudin, 1994). These two kinds of users will likely experience a product differently; both are relevant as test users.

- *End-user versus manager*: While the end-users operate the product, the managers oversee the end-users' work. Consequently, the end-users experience the product directly and have concrete knowledge about its use; the managers experience it indirectly and have more abstract knowledge about its use (Kensing and Munk-Madsen, 1993).

During early tests that focus on whether the product functionality meets user needs, it is highly relevant to include managers among the test users. During later tests that focus on refining the product design, end-users are the most relevant test users. If tests are conducted after user training has started, the test users should have completed this training; otherwise the product is tested with users who lack the agreed upon prerequisites for being users. That said, it might be prudent to include a couple of test users who have not had the training. Experience shows that in practice some users will often not get the training even though all users should in principle get it.

Yet another way of characterizing users is by the time at which they adopt new products. This characterization captures people's overall attitude toward new products as well as their influence on their peers' attitude toward new products (Rogers, 2003). *Innovators* are venturesome, like to try out new things, and are the first to adopt new products. They tend to interact mostly with other innovators. At the other end of the spectrum, *laggards* prefer the tried-and-tested solutions and mostly interact with others who also hold traditional values. They are the last to adopt a product. In between these two poles, there are three additional adopter categories: early adopters, early majority, and late majority, see Figure 5.1. The *early adopters* are more integrated in the local social context than the innovators; they are respected by their peers as the go-to persons for questions about new products. That is, they have a high degree of opinion leadership. The *early majority* adopts products before the average user and constitutes a numerous—and therefore important—category. They interact frequently with their peers but are seldom opinion leaders. The *late majority* is also a numerous category. They adopt products after the average user and often as the result of increasing peer pressure.

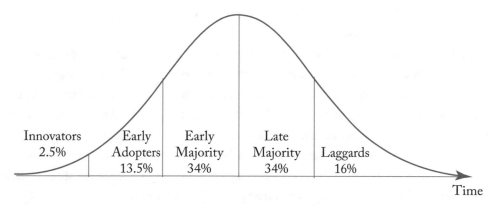

Figure 5.1: The five adopter categories, based on Rogers (2003). The innovators are, by definition, the first 2.5% to adopt a product (formally, the innovators are those users who adopt more than two standard deviations before the average user). The remaining adopter categories are similarly defined as a specified percentage of the total user population.

Innovators and early adopters are the adopter categories more likely to volunteer as test users. Innovators are rarely recruited, however. When they are, it is normally in an attempt to look into the future. The basis for these attempts is that innovators are considered to be "ahead of the trend" (von Hippel, 1986). That is, their experience with a product is considered indicative of how a broader group of users will experience the product when they at some future point are ready to adopt it. Like innovators, the early adopters are not representative of the average user. They are, for example, more innovation-minded and more forgiving toward usability problems. However, if they have served as test users, early adopters may spread the word about the product and their frequent opinion leadership adds weight to their words. In contrast, the late majority and laggards constitute half of the users but are unlikely to appear as test users unless actively recruited.

To get people to sign up as test users and actually have them show up for their session, you almost always need to provide an incentive. Money is a common incentive for test users external to the client company that commissions the test (Sova and Nielsen, 2003). You should ensure that these users receive an incentive commensurate with their time involvement. For test users internal to the client company, the incentives tend to be smaller and non-monetary. For both external and internal users, the use of monetary incentives may be complicated by national tax regulations or company policies. In addition, some people may be prohibited from receiving monetary incentives, yet still be relevant test users. Non-monetary incentives include gift cards (e.g., for bookstores or coffee shops), gifts (e.g., a product from the client company or a bottle of wine), and lunch (e.g., in the corporate cafeteria after the test session). You should keep in mind that some users do not read books, others do not drink alcohol, and so forth. It may pay to be creative. For example, Hockenberry and Blackburn (2016) had students with overdue library fines serve as test users of the library website in exchange for fine waivers.

Ideally, the recruitment of test users is done by random selection from user groups with carefully specified characteristics. The random selection and pre-specified user characteristics reduce bias and bolster the robustness and validity of the test. In practice, random selection is near impossible to achieve. Most usability tests are conducted with test users who satisfy some pre-specified user characteristics and were conveniently available. Convenience makes recruitment easier, but it should be remembered that the first eight people who respond to your invitation mail are exceedingly unlikely to constitute a representative sample of the user population. Still, their participation in your test may lead to the identification of many usability problems.

5.4   HOW MANY USERS ARE NEEDED?

It is well recognized that too few users is a serious threat to the robustness and completeness of a usability test. It is much more debated how many users are needed to counter this threat (Borsci et al., 2013; Nielsen and Landauer, 1993; Schmettow, 2012; Spool and Schroeder, 2001; Virzi, 1992). The most sensible answer to the question about how many users are needed is that "it depends." It depends on the following.

- The probability of encountering the usability problems: Is the product likely to have obvious usability problems or merely hard-to-find usability problems?

- The diversity of the target audience: Is there one homogeneous user group or multiple, heterogeneous user groups?

- The intended completeness of the test: Is the purpose of the test to find major usability problems or to find major as well as minor usability problems?

We will consider these three issues in turn.

The probability of encountering the usability problems: Most models for estimating the number of users needed in a usability test assume that the probability of encountering a usability problem in the tested product is known up front. This probability, λ, is formally defined as the probability of finding the average usability problem when running a single user. If the usability problems in the product are, on average, easy to come across, then λ should be set close to 1. This is for example the case when the current usability of the product is low. Conversely, if the usability problems in the product are, on average, difficult to find, then λ should be set close to 0. On the basis of λ, the proportion of usability problems found in a test with n users is given by Virzi (1992):

$$\text{Proportion of problems found} = 1 - (1 - \lambda)^n$$

Figure 5.2 graphs this formula for different values of λ. If the probability of finding the average usability problem when running a single user is 50% or more (i.e., $\lambda \geq .50$), then a usability test with five users will find more than 95% of the problems. In this situation, running more than five users will largely be wasted effort. The additional users will almost exclusively result in re-finding problems that were already found by running the first five users. However, this situation is rare. Setting λ to .50 (or more) corresponds to assuming that (at least) 50% of the problems have been found after running the first user. In most situations, this assumption is too optimistic. If you instead assume that 10% of the problems have been found after running the first user (i.e., $\lambda = .10$), then a usability test with five users will only find 41% of the problems, and you will need 29 users to find more than 95% of the problems. In this situation, the return on running, say, 15 rather than 5 users is a substantial increase in the proportion of problems found.

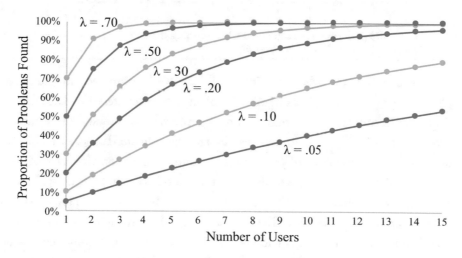

Figure 5.2: Estimated proportion of problems found in a usability test for different numbers of users and different probabilities of finding the problems.

Overall, Figure 5.2 shows that the number of users needed to find a given proportion of the problems depends heavily on λ. Without a good estimate of λ, the $1 - (1 - \lambda)^n$ formula is not of much use. It might be tempting to estimate λ on the basis of the first few users but doing so leads to overestimating λ and, thereby, underestimating the number of users to run (Lewis, 2001a). Table 5.3 shows a hypothetical example of a usability test with eight users, each of whom encountered 3–5 problems (indicated with an "×"). The eight users encountered a total of ten problems. After running the second user, six problems have been found (Problems #1, #3, #4, #5, #7, and #9). Thus, if we estimate λ (i.e., the average proportion of problems found by a single user) on the basis of the first two users we get: $\lambda_{estimate}$ = the average of 5/6 (1st user) and 3/6 (2nd user) = .67. This is a substantial overestimation compared to the value of .40 obtained after running all 8 users.

Table 5.3: Hypothetical results of a usability test with eight users

	Problems										Accumulated Problems	λ Estimate
	#1	#2	#3	#4	#5	#6	#7	#8	#9	#10		
1st User	×		×	×			×		×		5	1.00
2nd User	×			×	×						6	0.67
3rd User	×	×	×						×		7	0.57
4th User	×	×	×		×						7	0.57
5th User		×		×		×					8	0.48
6th User	×	×			×		×		×		8	0.50
7th User	×		×		×	×		×			9	0.46
8th User		×						×		×	10	0.40

Note: × indicates that the problem was encountered when running the user (e.g., running the 1st user led to the discovery of five problems (#1, #3, #4, #7, and #9).

Table 5.3 shows that the overestimation continues if λ is estimated after running the first three, four, five, six, or seven users because new problems are encountered by later users. Furthermore, running a ninth and tenth user may lead to the discovery of problems not encountered by any of the first eight users. That is, .40 may also be an overestimate. Turner et al. (2006) provide formulas for adjusting λ downward to get a more accurate estimate on the basis of the first few users. Schmettow (2012) argues that such adjustments are too uncertain to be useful in practice and, more generally, expresses "doubt that 80% of problems can be discovered with only 10 users" (p. 70).

The diversity of the target audience: The question about how many users to run in a usability test also depends on whether the target audience of the product is fairly homogeneous or consists of multiple, dissimilar user groups. If the target audience is fairly homogeneous, then there is a better chance that a test user from the target audience will encounter some of the same problems as any other person in the target audience. Conversely, if the target audience consists of dissimilar user groups, then a test user may encounter some of the same problems as any other person in the same user group, but these problems may be quite different from those encountered by persons from other user groups. Dating apps, e-government websites, and electronic health records are examples of products that have multiple user groups with different prerequisites.

The $1 - (1 - \lambda)^n$ formula assumes that any two users are equally likely to encounter any of the usability problems in the product. That is, it disregards the possibility of multiple, dissimilar user groups. When there are multiple, dissimilar user groups, then more users are needed. If the different user groups can be identified, then Caulton (2001) recommends running a usability test for each user group. For the electronic health record this recommendation amounts to, at least, six usability tests—one for the physicians, another for the nurses, and so forth. The number of users to run in each of these tests can be estimated using Figure 5.2.

It is also possible that you believe there are dissimilar user groups, but you cannot say how they should be defined. In this case, one option is to estimate the number of user groups, multiply this number with the number of users suggested by Figure 5.2, and randomly select this number of users from the target audience (Caulton, 2001). For example, if you estimate that there are seven user groups (without being able to specify their composition) and that eight users are needed to find 80% of the problems experienced by a user group (i.e., $\lambda \approx .20$), then run 56 randomly selected users.

The intended completeness of the test: While completeness is an attractive property of a usability test, it must be balanced against its cost in time and other resources. In the development of a multi-million-dollar system, the cost of running 40–80 users may be negligible. In an upgrade of the company intranet, Caulton's (2001) recommendations quickly become unrealizable when the number of user groups increases. Another way of looking at Figure 5.2 is to use it for estimating how *few* users are needed to find enough problems to make the test worthwhile. A test is worthwhile if running it is preferable to proceeding without testing. Even with the modest assumption that the average problem has a 10% chance of being encountered when running a single user, a usability test with just four users will find one third of the problems (provided the target audience is fairly homogeneous). While this is far from completeness, it shows that a small amount of usability testing goes a long way.

In assessing the level of completeness necessary to make a test worthwhile, it is important to consider whether the test is summative or formative. Completeness is central to summative tests, which seek to give an accurate and balanced picture of the usability of a product. It is less important in formative tests because their completeness must be weighed against other considerations.

- The resources required to run and analyze a usability test increase with the number of users. A high level of completeness may require more users than the usability budget allows for analysis. If so, a test with fewer users may still provide valuable usability insights.

- The number of problems that can be fixed in response to a test influences how many problems it makes sense to identify during the test. If the development schedule merely allocates a week for fixing the identified problems, then there is no need for a test that identifies so many problems that it will take a month to fix them (Wixon, 2003).

- The revisions made to fix a problem may introduce a new problem or render a hitherto invisible problem visible. By implication, the revisions made to fix many problems may substantially change the usability issues that remain in a product. Thus, one high-completeness test followed by one extensive revision cycle may produce a product with many remaining usability problems.

For these reasons, it makes practical sense to identify and fix a manageable number of problems and then conduct a new usability test (Hartson and Pyla, 2012; Nielsen, 1993). The new test serves to evaluate whether the revisions were successful and to identify additional usability problems that were missed in the first test. In such an iterative design process, the series of usability tests should—ideally—find the complete set of usability problems. The individual usability test should not.

5.5   MAKE TASKS

The test tasks serve three purposes. First, they prescribe what the users should try to achieve with the product. The particulars of the tasks ensure that the users exercise the product in concrete detail. Without these particulars, the users would engage with the product for no other purpose than exploring it; the resulting test would be superficial. In addition, most users are uncertain about what it entails to participate in a usability test. The tasks help reduce this uncertainty by clarifying to the users what they are to do.

Second, the tasks focus the test on specified parts of the product. Most products have more features than it is possible to cover in a single usability test. Thus, it is necessary to decide which features to include in the test. Multiple criteria enter into this decision. For example, some features may be more central to the product than others; some features may be more in need of testing than others; and some features may be ready for testing, while others do not yet exist. Once it has been decided which features to include in the test, the tasks convey this decision to the test users.

Third, the tasks provide a goal against which the evaluator can assess the users' actions. Knowing the users' tasks makes it possible for the evaluator to: (1) follow what the users try to accomplish with their actions; (2) know what they should do to make progress; (3) realize when they are off track; (4) spot whether they overlook information needed for the task; (5) assess how closely their task solution matches the task particulars; and (6) appreciate why they find the product easy, frustrating, fun, tedious, rewarding, or disappointing to use.

With respect to their content, test tasks may be more or less specific. If user needs have not yet been clarified, then the functionality of the product is still fluid and it is premature to decide on a list of specific tasks. Any list of specific tasks risks targeting product functionality that later turns out to be irrelevant as well as risks missing tasks that later emerge as important. This situation is common when usability tests are conducted early in the development process. In this situation, the usability test should help clarify the user needs.

Open-ended test tasks serve this purpose, see Figure 5.3 for an example. Open-ended tasks are also popular in later tests that focus on the users' emotions, engagement, generic experience, and the like rather than on identifying usability problems (Bargas-Avila and Hornbæk, 2011). With open-ended tasks, the users should be free to explore and imagine how the product may support them and improve their experience. The tasks should impose as few constraints as possible. For example, the nurses in the test of the Round application (Figure 5.3) are neither presented with situational details, nor given a goal to achieve. Instead, they are invited to bring their real-world experience to bear on the prototype. Because open-ended tasks are mostly used early in the development process, the prototype will often be low fidelity; thus, it too is open-ended. There is no right or wrong solution to an open-ended task. The users are set loose and the evaluator simply needs to be attentive to their feedback. In terms of preparations, familiarity with the domain is crucial to the evaluator's ability to appreciate and follow up on this feedback.

Usability Test of the Round Application

You have just arrived at your workplace and you begin to prepare your work shift. Round is a new application that you can use during your work. (You have already logged in.)

Figure 5.3: Example of open-ended test task, based on Tarkkanen and Harkke (2019). The Round application is an interface-only prototype of a mobile app that provides nurses with access to the electronic patient record at the hospital.

If the usability test is conducted after the user needs have, more or less, been clarified, then the test tasks should be specific. Specific tasks are fictional situations, see Figure 5.4. To help the user imagine the situation, the task list may be preceded by a scenario that sets the scene for the tasks. Each task is specified in concrete detail to enable—or gently force—the user to solve the task with reference to a realistically complex situation. Without the specific details, it is for example likely that the users in the test of the U-Haul website (Figure 5.4) would not care much about the size of the moving truck but simply rent any truck. If so, the test would skip over an element that the U-Haul website aims to support because sufficient size is crucial to a real user's experience with a rented moving truck.

In making specific tasks, the evaluator should also solve them and specify their solution. Obviously, the solution should not be given to the test users; it is intended to help the evaluator assess the users' actions by providing a point of reference. The evaluator may also consider to include a task that cannot be solved with the tested product (Cordes, 2001). In the real world, it is not uncommon for users to be uncertain whether a product can be used for solving a task. It may be relevant to test how users establish that a task is unsolvable with the tested product, how certain they are, and whether they find that the product ought to support the task.

Usability Test of the U-Haul Website

Your friends Mike and Anna are about to move from Pittsburgh, PA, to Denver, CO. They have an apartment in Pittsburgh consisting of a living room, a bedroom, a kitchen, and a bathroom. They want to find the cheapesst service for the move to Colorado. They expect to make the move themselves with some help from a few friends.

Task 1: The couple needs a truck that is suitable for all the furniture and belongings in their three-room apartment. Please find the total price the couple will have to pay for the truck. Note: they are moving on April 14th from Darlington Rd. in Pittsburgh, PA, 15217, to Emerson St. in Denver, CO 80218.

A 17' truck is required. The price of the truck is $1,213, plus SafeMove insurance $105, plus environmental fee $5. Taxes are not included. The tax rate does not seem to be available from the website.

Task 2: Before you go any further, you want to check if Mike and Anna need a special driver's license to drive the truck across country. Where would you find that info?

Figure 5.4: Example of specific test tasks, based on Hertzum et al. (2014). The example shows the test scenario, two (of seven) tasks, and the solution (in italics) for the first task. In the usability test, you would give the test user the scenario and the tasks but not the solution; the solution is only for the evaluator. U-Haul is an operational website for renting moving trucks.

Irrespective of their specificity, the test tasks should be brief and in plain language. Keeping the tasks in plain language includes using words that are natural to the user, rather than adopting the terms that appear in the user interface of the tested product. Otherwise, the tasks short-circuit an important part of the test, namely whether the users are able to relate the terms in the user interface to their tasks. It is also important that the wording of the tasks does not give hints as to the required user actions. For example, the scenario and first task in Figure 5.4 describe the amount of furniture and belongings in the couple's apartment; it is left for the user to realize that this information implies the need of estimating which size of truck to rent. Furthermore, the tasks should preferably be available in writing so that the users can refer back to them whenever needed. Presenting the tasks one at a time helps the users in staying focused on the current task. Starting with an easy task reduces the stress often felt by test users.

The quality and relevance of the tasks matter. With increasing task quality and task relevance, a usability test tends to identify more usability problems (Skov and Stage, 2012). Thus, the work that goes into making good test tasks pays off. In testing products for international use, this work includes that you must customize the test tasks to local usage patterns. For example, Barnum (2011) describes that Chinese users of automatic teller machines (ATMs) prefer to take out all of their salary for a month in one withdrawal, while Western users might stop at an ATM frequently to withdraw enough cash for a day or an event. This difference in usage patterns calls for differences in the test tasks, even though the tested product is the same for both user groups. Importantly, these user groups do not necessarily live in different countries. The international users of a product include immigrants, sojourners, and tourists.

Lindgaard and Chattratichart (2007) find that the number of severe problems identified increases with the number of test tasks. This finding reflects that a test with more tasks can cover more product features. However, it also accentuates the tradeoff between the number of tasks and the length of the test sessions. Typically, sessions are limited to little more than an hour to avoid that user fatigue produces misleading test results. Depending on the characteristics of the tasks, this limit allows for something like 5–10 tasks. In estimating how long it will take users to solve the tasks, time must be included for the users to understand the tasks, explore the product, recover from mistakes, think aloud, and answer any post-task questions.

5.6   SET UP EQUIPMENT

Usability tests can be conducted with nearly no equipment. A notebook for recording usability problems and user comments may be enough for a low-cost test that primarily seeks to identify glaring problems. Such a setup has the advantage of extreme flexibility. That said, additional equipment for recording the test sessions can dramatically improve the robustness, completeness, and impact of a usability test, provided the recordings are viewed during the analysis phase. If you do not have the time to view the recordings, you should not make them but focus on thorough note-taking instead. Three kinds of recording equipment are especially worth considering in setting up a usability test.

- *Screen-recording apps*, which capture the content of the product screen as it evolves in response to user interactions.

- *Audio and video recorders*, which capture the users' behavior, verbalizations, body language, and facial expressions.

- *Logging apps*, in which the evaluator can type free-text notes and click buttons to indicate the occurrence of pre-defined events.

Screen-recording apps are available for laptops, phones, and the like but not for all the other kinds of products that may also be subject to usability testing. By being internal to the computer, such apps always have a full view of the screen, something that is often difficult to achieve with an external camera. External cameras are versatile because they can be used to record anything, but many users perceive it as stressful to be video recorded (Schrier, 1992). If the users become self-aware or are otherwise not at ease, then they behave unnaturally. This unnaturalness reduces the validity of the test. Most logging apps can be linked to a screen or video recording. In this case, the evaluator can designate a button to indicate the presence of usability problems. Clicking the button will then log the timestamp at which the problem occurred and, thereby, make it easy to return to this point in the screen or video recording during analysis. Other buttons may be set up to log when the users make hedonic expressions, when they start on a new task, and so forth.

A mundane element of the test equipment is the general look and feel of the location in which the test is conducted—the lab. In spite of its name, the lab may be a company conference room, a hotel meeting room, or some other space; it need not be a laboratory in any formal sense. To reduce its artificialness, the lab should be equipped with the most critical components of the real use context. This may include home-like décor when testing leisure products, office furniture when testing business systems, and different setups for tests with children as opposed to adults. Further contextual factors are also important to the validity of the test. Such factors include having everyday materials and tools available during the sessions and simulating interruptions and time pressures if they will be frequent during real use (Bødker and Madsen, 1998).

Traditionally, usability labs were divided into a test room and an observation room, separated by a one-way mirror (Dumas and Redish, 1999). The users were in the test room and could neither see nor hear what went on in the observation room. The evaluator and other spectators, such as the product developers, sat in the observation room from which they could see and hear the users. The rationale for the traditional lab was to avoid influencing the users. While some still consider this issue paramount, others loathe the associated formality. Generally, the proponents of the traditional lab are testing the utilitarian, as opposed to experiential, aspects of product use.

Those who loathe the traditional lab find that with the evaluator and users in separate rooms it becomes impossibly hard for the evaluator to facilitate the users in talking eloquently about their user experience. They recommend that tests are conducted in single-room labs with no observation room. Having the evaluator in the test room with the user is, for example, preferable in early usability tests that aim to clarify user requirements, in tests with low-fidelity prototypes that require interventions from the evaluator, and in tests with users who need much assistance or prompting. That is, the decision about whether the evaluator should be beside or separated from the user depends on three factors (Dumas and Loring, 2008): the objective of the test, the fidelity of the prototype, and the characteristics of the users.

In tests of websites and the like, the relevance of the traditional lab is fading; it is increasingly found wanting in both cost-effectiveness and mobility (Sharma, 2013). Usability tests are increasingly made with mobile equipment in single-room locations, such as meeting rooms. Furthermore, the spectators in the observation room of the traditional lab may raise ethical issues. In particular, Wilson (2007) notes that the users' managers should not be allowed to observe the test sessions.

CHAPTER 6

Execution: Running the Test Sessions

Running a usability test consists of completing a series of test sessions, one for each user. A test session begins when the user arrives to the lab and ends when the user departs from it. Between these two end points are several activities.

- *Welcoming and instructing the users,* including how to make the users feel at ease (Section 6.1).

- *Observing users and listening in on their thoughts,* including how to become sensitized to what they do and say (Section 6.2).

- *Prompting users when needed,* including considerations about how and how much to prompt (Section 6.3).

- *Taking notes,* including how evaluators manage to attend to test-session moderation, on-the-fly analysis as well as note-taking (Section 6.4).

- *Asking post-task questions,* including examples of standard instruments for gauging the users' perception of common user-experience constructs (Section 6.5).

- *Thanking the user at* the end of the test session (Section 6.6).

Table 6.1: Checklist – execution

- ☐ The users have given their informed consent to take part in the test
- ☐ The users have been put at their ease before they start working on the test tasks
- ☐ The users have been instructed in what to do, including how to think aloud
- ☐ The evaluator has a rich repertoire of constructs and sensitizing questions for noticing how the users experience the product
- ☐ The evaluator has restricted prompting to affirmations (classic thinking aloud) or also prompted the users about their experience and reflections (relaxed thinking aloud)
- ☐ When providing assistance, the evaluator has preferred general hints to specific hints and aimed to restrict the provided information to the current step of the test task
- ☐ To complement the recordings of the sessions, or in place of recordings, the evaluator has taken notes of events of interest
- ☐ After a task, the evaluator has returned to any outstanding issues to ask the user for clarification
- ☐ If all users are asked predetermined post-task questions, then these questions have been worded carefully or standard questionnaire instruments have been used
- ☐ The evaluator has thanked the users for participating in the test and explained to them that their efforts to solve the tasks are valuable input to the usability test

Table 6.1 provides a checklist for the execution of the test sessions. Evaluators may run through the checklist shortly before each session to remind themselves of issues they must keep in mind during the sessions. Or, evaluators may every now and then walk through the checklist shortly after a session to learn whether some of its items warrant their renewed attention.

6.1   WELCOME AND INSTRUCT USERS

When the users arrive for their test sessions, they likely know little about what is going to happen. They may also be slightly anxious about whether they will be able to do alright. Users with little interest in technology (e.g., late majority and laggards, see Section 5.3) may worry that they do not know enough about technology to fulfil their role as test users. Users with a strong interest in technology may worry that they will lose face by not appearing as technology savvy as they would like to appear. It is therefore important to take time to put the user at ease. For this purpose, the evaluator should:

- thank the user for agreeing to take part in the test;

- describe the objective of the test in general terms;

- introduce the user to the test room and its equipment; and

- introduce the product or prototype that will be tested.

The underlying theme in these explanations should be to convey to the user that the session is a test of the product, not of the user. It should also be explained to the users that they should merely express how they personally experience the product. They are not expected to account for the thoughts and views of, for example, their colleagues. There will be other sessions in which other users express their experience, and the outcome of the test is the aggregate of all the sessions.

In putting the users at ease, it is important to heed their cultural background (Barnum, 2011; Clemmensen et al., 2009; Frandsen-Thorlacius et al., 2009). When the user and evaluator have similar cultural backgrounds, they tacitly rely on shared cultural habits and manners of speech, such as shared metaphors. When their cultural backgrounds differ, the user and evaluator do not have a shared repertoire of cultural habits and manners of speech. In these cases, you need to devote more time and attention to establish a test situation in which the users comment freely on the product.

An example of a cultural issue is whether the users have a task focus or a socio-emotional focus. People with a task focus direct their efforts toward task-related goals and focus their attention on monitoring the extent to which these goals are being accomplished. Thus, these users' perception of the evaluator may not influence their behavior appreciably, because they just focus on the test tasks. In contrast, people with a socio-emotional focus direct their effort and attention toward the interpersonal climate of the situation and strive to maintain social harmony. These users may be influenced by their perception of the evaluator's status and may react to subtle cues in the evaluator's behavior. A task focus is common among people with a Western cultural background, whereas a socio-emotional focus is common among people with an Eastern cultural background (Clemmensen et al., 2009).

To formalize their participation in the test, the users should sign an informed-consent form, see Figure 6.1. Informed consent is about protecting the users' rights as well as the rights of the company conducting the test (Burmeister, 2000). The users' rights include that they should receive information about the test, that this information should be comprehensible to them, that their participation in the test should be voluntary, that the data collected about them should be kept confident, and that the test sessions should involve minimal risk to the users. Minimal risk means that "the probability and magnitude of harm is no greater than that encountered in the daily lives of all (or the great majority) of persons in the population from which research subjects are to be recruited" (Weijer, 2000, p. 359).

The rights of the company conducting the test include that the users should not discuss the tested product outside of the test session. Such non-disclosure clauses are needed If participation in the test involves working with sensitive information, such as commercially sensitive information about new products or personally sensitive information about real persons who feature in system data. In addition, the users may grant the company restricted or full rights to the data collected about them. Restricted rights mean that the company may use the data for the purposes of the test only. Full rights mean that the users also grant the company the rights to use the data for other purposes, such as in the training of new evaluators.

When products are usability tested after an organization has started using them, the test users are often people internal to the organization. Such usability tests may provide pertinent input for product revisions, but they pose special challenges for informed consent (Burmeister and Weckert, 2003). For example, it may be questioned whether the test users' participation is voluntary. Some will argue that the terms of employment are sufficient to require that employees participate in a usability test or, at least, that they can be expected to participate if their employer asks them. Even if internals are formally told that their participation is voluntary, there will likely be covert pressure to agree to participate and to remain until the end. Confidentiality also becomes a thornier issue with internal users. Internal users may worry that it will be possible to deduce their identity from the final test report, that unflattering stories about the problems they experience will leak to their colleagues, or that their test data will become available to their manager and possibly seen as indicative of their job qualifications. These worries increase if the test sessions are recorded or if they are observed by spectators other than the evaluator. To put the users, especially internal users, at ease, you must address such issues directly and up front.

Informed Consent

Usability test of: [NAME OF TESTED PRODUCT]

Purpose: The goal of this test is to evaluate how users experience the tested product. As a test user, you will be asked to use the product for solving a number of tasks, while you think out loud. During and after the tasks, you will be prompted for additional information about your experience with the product.

Comprehension: At the beginning of the test, you are informed about the purpose and procedure of the test. By signing this form, you indicate that you have received and understood this information.

Risk: You may become fatigued during the test. If so, you will be given the opportunity to rest. There are no other risks associated with your participation in the test.

Voluntariness: You are free to withdraw from the test at any time. Withdrawal does not incur prejudice or penalty of any kind. You are not obliged to provide a reason for withdrawing.

Nondisclosure: Because the product has not yet been released, you cannot discuss its features or your experience using them in the test for a period of 12 months after the test.

Confidentiality: All information collected during the test will be kept confidential. Unless you tick the box below, no information that may identify you will be viewed by people other than the evaluation team.

☐ I grant [COMPANY NAME] permission to use excerpts of the video and audio of my test session in the communication of test results and in the training of test evaluators.

_____   _____   _____
        User's Name   Signature   Date

_____   _____   _____
      Evaluator's Name   Signature   Date

Figure 6.1: Informed-consent form; based on Burmeister (2000), Lazar et al. (2010), and Wilson (2007).

Finally, the users should be instructed in thinking aloud. Thinking aloud is an artificial thing to do; users do not do it during their day-to-day use of products. It is, however, an effective means of making the users' thoughts available to the evaluator and, therefore, an important component in usability tests. To implement thinking aloud, the users should provide a running commentary of their thought process. The instructions about how to think aloud should exemplify the kinds of thoughts the users should verbalize. Depending on the objective of the test, the users may be instructed to:

- verbalize their deliberations about how the product works, their uncertainty about how to make progress on the tasks, their appreciation of the interface aesthetics, their frustration with specific product features, their expectations about what the product would support them in doing, and any other aspect important to their experience of using the product; or

- verbalize the task information they attend to, the sub goal they currently seek to accomplish, the interface objects they examine to match the sub goal to the available options, the information they infer from user-interface feedback, the answers they obtain for sub goals, and the conclusions they draw about whether they are making progress toward task completion.

While the former includes a rich set of reflections on how the users experience the product, the latter is restricted to the information that enters into performing the tasks. Hertzum et al. (2009) refer to these two forms of thinking aloud as relaxed thinking aloud and classic thinking aloud, respectively. Relaxed thinking aloud focuses on the experiential aspects of product use and is suited for tests that prioritize these aspects over the utilitarian aspects of product use. Conversely, classic thinking aloud focuses on the utilitarian aspects of product use. However, it can be used for a broad range of usability tests, provided the evaluator is prepared to infer the users' experiential reactions from observing them and listening to their utilitarian verbalizations. One advantage of classic thinking aloud is that it comes with fewer validity issues than relaxed thinking aloud, see Section 6.3. In instructing the users about how to think aloud, it is effective to complement an oral instruction with showing the users a video snippet of a person who thinks aloud in the requested way.

6.2   OBSERVE USERS AND LISTEN IN ON THEIR THOUGHTS

Observing the users and listening in on their thoughts are bottom-up activities, which should be driven by what the users actually do and say. It is, however, not easy to see and hear what goes on right in front of you. Button and Sharrock (2009) consider it so difficult that their first rule for making observation is: "open your eyes." The meaning of this rule is that something is going on; the tricky part is to notice it. To notice what goes on, the evaluator needs a rich repertoire of constructs for thinking about how users experience products. With increasing richness in your repertoire of constructs, you can make still finer distinctions and, thereby, notice more and more aspects of the user experience (Hertzum and Clemmensen, 2012).

The ISO 9241 (2010) definition of usability alerts the evaluator to the three dimensions of effectiveness, efficiency, and satisfaction (Section 2.1). With increasing knowledge and experience, these three dimensions get subdivided into many more constructs. Hertzum and Clemmensen (2012) find that 19% of usability professionals' usability constructs are about effectiveness, 21% about efficiency, and 13% about satisfaction. The constructs about effectiveness for example include distinctions about relational aspects (e.g., "Working alone to produce a product" vs. "For fun with people I know"). However, Hertzum and Clemmensen (2012) also find that 47% of usability professionals' usability constructs are not about effectiveness, efficiency, and satisfaction. Evaluators need additional constructs to perform their work competently. A large part of these additional constructs are experiential constructs beyond satisfaction, including constructs about visual aesthetics, creative expression, personalization, and fashionableness.

To become sensitized to how test users experience a product, the evaluator needs ideas about what to look for, listen for, and pay attention to. The objective of the test provides such ideas, as does familiarity with the domain, prototype, and test tasks. As described above, ideas also come from the evaluator's repertoire of constructs for thinking about usability and user experience. Still other ideas may come from sensitizing questions. Sensitizing questions are questions that evaluators may ask themselves to open their eyes, and other senses, more fully to what goes on during a test session. They are neither questions posed to the users (but by the evaluators to themselves), nor intended as a scheme to be followed in any strict sense. Rather, evaluators can turn to sensitizing questions when they feel a need to stimulate their capacity for noticing what is going on.

Table 6.2 gives sensitizing questions for the utilitarian aspect of the user experience. These questions are most relevant when the test employs specific tasks (Section 5.5) and require that the evaluator knows the steps involved in solving the tasks. The questions are derived from the user action framework (Andre et al., 2001), which in turn builds on Norman's (1986) seven-stage model of how users perform a task. According to this model, product use is a goal-directed activity. Users start off with a goal—a task—expressed in user terms. To achieve this goal, they need to convert it into a sequence of interactions with the product. The first three stages are about this conversion, which involves that the users determine the general requirements for achieving the goal, decompose it into sub goals, and specify the action necessary to achieve each sub goal. For each stage, a sensitizing question seeks to alert the evaluator to the specific kind of difficulty that users may possibly experience at that stage. The fourth stage is the execution of the actions. It may involve difficulties such as pressing small buttons, completing actions within narrow timeframes, and remembering information obtained earlier in the interaction sequence. The three last stages are about determining whether the executed action produced progress toward the successful completion of the task. During these stages, the users perceive, interpret, and evaluate the feedback received from the product. Or they fail to notice it, cannot understand it, or remain uncertain whether they made progress.

Table 6.2: Sensitizing questions for the utilitarian aspect of the user experience, based on Andre et al. (2001)

Stage	Description	Sensitizing Question
High-level planning	Establishing the goal	Can the user determine the general requirements for performing the task?
Intention	Decomposing the goal into sub goals	Does the user try to achieve the right sub goal (or are sub goals dropped or out of sequence)?
Action specification	Specifying the action needed to achieve sub goal	Can the user determine what action to perform to achieve the sub goal?
Execution	Executing the action	Can the user perform the action easily and accurately?
Perception	Perceiving the system state resulting from the action	Does the user notice the feedback?
Interpretation	Making sense of the system state	Does the user understand the feedback?
Evaluation	Evaluating the system state with respect to the goal	Can the user determine whether progress has been made toward completing the task?

While the utilitarian aspect of product use is relevant to a vast number of usability tests, other tests are equally or more about the experiential aspect. Table 6.3 gives sensitizing questions for the experiential aspect of the user experience. These questions are derived from the customer-experience framework by Gentile et al. (2007). They find that users' experiences of products have multiple components, but they also point out that users more likely experience these components as a unitary feeling than as separate components. Thus, the sensitizing questions associated with the components apply to overlapping parts of the users' product interactions—in contrast to the questions in Table 6.2, which relate to distinct stages in a process. The sensitizing questions about the experiential aspect of the user experience alert the evaluator to the multiple ways in which a product may have value to users: sensorial, emotional, cognitive, pragmatic, lifestyle, and relational. For example, products associated with lifestyle-related user experiences touch on values that are important to the users' identity and ways of presenting themselves toward others. Getting this component right may create loyal, long-term customers. Hertzum and Clemmensen (2012) find that usability professionals' usability constructs are distributed across all six experiential components.

Table 6.3: Sensitizing questions for the experiential aspect of the user experience, based on Gentile et al. (2007)

Component	Description	Sensitizing Question
Sensorial	Stimulating the senses of sight, hearing, touch, taste, and smell	Does the product arouse aesthetic pleasure, excitement, joy, a sense of beauty, or their opposites?
Emotional	Affecting the users by generating moods, feelings, and emotions	Does the product generate an emotional experience and thereby an affective relation with the product, brand, or company?
Cognitive	Involving the users in thinking or in conscious mental processes	Does the product engage the users in using their creativity, in problem solving, or may it lead the users to revise their usual ideas and assumptions?
Pragmatic	The practical act of doing something	Does the product enable the users to do something or express themselves easily and accurately?
Lifestyle	Affirming the users' beliefs and system of values	Can the product be a means of adhesion to certain values or of affirming a social identity or lifestyle?
Relational	Embracing the users' social context and relationships with other people	Does the product encourage use together with other people, can it become the core of a shared passion, or may it foster community building?

6.3   PROMPT USERS WHEN NEEDED

To make their thoughts accessible to the evaluator, the users are requested to think aloud while they solve the test tasks. However, the users will occasionally fall silent, for example to concentrate on the tasks. In addition, some users simply verbalize less than others. If the users' silence lasts for more than about 30 seconds, then they should be prompted to resume thinking aloud. The users may also be prompted for their thoughts on specific issues that the evaluator considers important to understanding their user experience. However, such prompts risk distracting the users or otherwise influencing their performance of the tasks. That is, they involve a validity risk, which must be weighed against the value of the information obtained.

Ericsson and Simon (1993) distinguish among three levels of thinking aloud and contend that the two first levels do not alter the users' behavior and thought process in any other way than by prolonging it. In contrast, the third level alters the users' thought process and thereby possibly their manner of solving the tasks (Ericsson and Simon, 1993; Fox et al., 2011; Hertzum et al., 2009). The three levels of thinking aloud are as follows.

- *Level 1*: the verbalization of thoughts and information that are already in the user's present focus of attention in verbal form. No extra processing is needed to report these thoughts and users need expend no special effort to communicate them. Level 1 verbalizations for example include verbalizing the attended snippets of on-screen text, the menu items considered for selection, the labels of followed links, and the information to be typed into input fields or remembered for later use.

- *Level 2*: the verbalization of information that is presently in the user's focus of attention but in nonverbal form, including images and abstract concepts. While such information must be recoded into verbal form to be reported, this recoding does not bring new information into the user's focus of attention. The task in Figure 5.4 provides an example. In estimating the size of the moving truck needed for that task, the user may scan a mental image of her flat to get a sense of the amount of furniture and, in that process, verbalize the pieces of furniture that appear in the image.

- *Level 3*: the verbalization of thoughts beyond those occasioned by task performance. These verbalizations influence the user's focus of attention by requiring that the user links present thoughts to earlier thoughts, which are thereby brought back into the user's focus of attention. For example, users make level 3 verbalizations when they are asked to explain their behavior, to express what feedback they expect from the product, or to state whether their experience is pleasurable or frustrating.

Ericsson and Simon (1993) recommend restricting thinking aloud to verbalizations at levels 1 and 2. The reason for this recommendation is that level 3 verbalizations alter the users' thought process and, thereby, influence their behavior and experience. Verbalizing at levels 1 and 2 only is the definition of classic thinking aloud (Hertzum et al., 2009). It focuses on the utilitarian aspects of product use. In contrast, relaxed thinking aloud encompasses verbalizations at all three levels. It constitutes a relaxation of the thinking-aloud protocol recommended by Ericsson and Simon (1993) and yields first-hand verbalizations about the experiential aspects of product use. The choice of either classic or relaxed thinking aloud should reflect the objective of the usability test. In their survey of usability-test practices, McDonald et al. (2012) find that relaxed thinking aloud is the more common choice. Once made, this choice has implications for how to instruct the users in thinking aloud and how to prompt them while they solve the tasks.

A standard phrase in classic thinking aloud is to instruct the user to "act as if you are alone in the room speaking to yourself" (Ericsson and Simon, 1993, p. 376). This instruction can be reinforced by a usability lab divided into a test room and an observation room (Section 5.6). The rationale for this instruction is straightforward: It is easier for the users to maintain an exclusive focus on task information (i.e., verbalization at levels 1 and 2) if they do not think of themselves as involved in a conversation with the evaluator. In line with the instruction to the users, the evaluator should largely remain silent and only prompt the users in ways designed to keep them talking. Specifically, the users should be reminded to resume talking if they have not been verbalizing for some time. You may for example use the neutral prompt "keep talking."

Asking the users to pretend that they are alone in the room has, however, been criticized for making the situation artificial. For example, Boren and Ramey (2000) consider it counterproductive to assume that verbalizations can be divorced from communicative purposes. If it is, instead, acknowledged that the evaluator and user are communicating, then it becomes important that you design your prompts to create and maintain a highly asymmetrical speaker/listener relationship in which the users talk and you listen. Affirmations such as "okay," "mm hm," and "uh-huh" are particularly useful for this purpose. According to speech communication theory, listeners make affirmations at the end of a speaker's conversational units to indicate that they follow what the speaker has said so far and wish for the speaker to continue with the next unit (Boren and Ramey, 2000). That is, affirmations serve the double purpose of indicating engaged listening and simultaneously indicating that the listener foregoes the opportunity to assume speakership. If you make good use of affirmations, then the communication with the users will proceed in accordance with deeply rooted conversational conventions. Consequently, the users will do nearly all the talking without experiencing the situation as overly artificial.

Affirmations are also highly useful in relaxed thinking aloud. However, in relaxed thinking aloud the evaluator also asks questions. Hertzum and Kristoffersen (2018) investigated what the evaluator says while the users are solving the test tasks. They found that 38% of the evaluator's verbalizations are affirmations, 32% are instructions about the tasks, 16% are prompts for reflection, 5% are assistance in solving the tasks, 4% are prompts for description, and 6% are other verbalizations. The prompts for reflection are the clearest indication of relaxed thinking aloud (in classic thinking aloud the vast majority of the evaluator's verbalizations should be affirmations). The prompts for reflection include asking the users to (Hertzum and Kristoffersen, 2018):

- state their impression of the product, for example "Do you think that was easy or difficult to find?"

- express their expectations, for example "So what would you expect there?"

- elaborate verbalizations they made earlier, for example "So, is that what you thought when you mentioned they would want to [be able to do X]?"

- indicate whether they noticed specific pieces of information, for example "Did you see any options for choosing [X] when you placed the order?"

- take specific actions to clarify something for the evaluator, for example "Why don't you take a look at the shopping cart and show me where you would expect it to show up?"

- explain whether they interpreted a situation in one way or another, for example "Do you think that even though there is no insurance they still might not have to pay all of it, or is something automatically included and you said no to extra insurance?"

The two last examples invite the users to reflect further on issues they may have glossed over fairly quickly. Such prompts should be used with caution. They may be valuable when the users appear to have missed or misunderstood something and the evaluator wants to probe the extent of the misunderstanding. These prompts border on providing assistance and must be expected to influence the users' behavior and experience. To avoid leading or biasing the users, the prompts should generally take the form of open questions, such as "What would you do next?" or "Tell me what you think of that task" (Dumas and Loring, 2008). Open questions merely invite the users to share their thoughts. In contrast, closed questions suggest a fixed focus or set of response options. Thereby, the user's subsequent verbalization is largely reduced to a confirmation or disconfirmation of the evaluator's reading of the situation. Closed questions should only be used when the evaluator wants information about something specific, such as "Do you think that is a relevant function?"

It may be tempting to construe a usability test with relaxed thinking aloud as a kind of interview. It is not (Hertzum, 2016). In interviews, the users can talk about a product and their experiences with it, but their talking is detached from concrete product use. In contrast, the users in a usability test exercise the product; their behavior and verbalizations relate to their use of the product for solving the test tasks. Thus, the relation between the users and the product is different in that the usability test maintains a focus on concrete product use. Furthermore, an interviewer relies on the users' verbalizations for information about their behavior and experience, whereas the evaluator in a usability test observes the users' behavior directly and prompts them for complementary information about the unobservable aspects of the user experience.

Zhao and McDonald (2010) find that for both classic and relaxed thinking aloud causal explanations, problem formulations, and recommendations are the three categories with the highest percentages of relevant user verbalizations, see Figure 6.2. In contrast, the three most frequent categories were action description, reading out text and links, and result evaluation. A total of 83% (classic) and 73% (relaxed) of the users' verbalizations were in these three categories, but they included few verbalizations relevant to the identification of usability problems. Figure 6.2 also exemplifies that it is difficult for users to restrict their verbalizations to classic thinking aloud: Users instructed to do classic thinking aloud also make causal explanations, problem formulations, and recommendations. These categories are level 3 verbalizations and thus go beyond classic thinking aloud (Hertzum et al., 2015).

Classic Thinking Aloud	Category	Relaxed Thinking Aloud
100%	Causal Explanation	88%
86%	Problem Formulation	82%
57%	Recommendation	27%
23%	User Experience	24%
15%	Impact on Outcomes	8%
7%	Result Evaluation	8%
6%	Action Explanation	7%
1%	Action Description	1%
1%	Reading	1%
100% 75% 50% 25% 0%		0% 25% 50% 75% 100%

Figure 6.2: Percentage of user verbalizations relevant to the identification of usability problems for different categories of user verbalizations, based on Zhao and McDonald (2010).

Talking is slower than thinking. Consequently, thinking aloud slows the users down and should not be combined with the measurement of task completion times. Fox et al. (2011) found that the slowdown differs for classic and relaxed thinking aloud. During classic thinking aloud, the users perform tasks more slowly but in the same way they might perform them when they are not verbalizing. Thus, their strategies for solving a task and their execution of it are unaltered. During relaxed thinking aloud, the users perform tasks differently when they think aloud. They have, for example, been found to issue more commands for navigating both within and among webpages, to spend a larger part of tasks on distributed visual behavior, and to experience higher mental workload (Hertzum et al., 2009). In addition, the users are asked to provide reasons for their actions during relaxed thinking aloud. Providing such reasons may shift their focus from the selection of the option perceived to be most promising toward the selection of the option supported by the best reasons.

The effect of thinking aloud on the users' behavior also varies with their cultural background. Kim (2002) found that users with a cultural background from East Asia solved more tasks incorrectly when thinking aloud than when performing without thinking aloud. In contrast, users with a Western cultural background were not impaired by thinking aloud; they even appeared to perform better while thinking aloud than when they were requested to perform in silence. Thus, when the test users have different cultural backgrounds, it must be assumed that thinking aloud affects some test users' performance and that different users are affected differently.

If a usability problem occurs early in a task, then it may block the user's progress and prevent the discovery of additional problems later in the task. To reach the later part of a task, the evaluator may assist the user who experiences an early usability problem, once it has been discovered that the user is stuck. In providing assistance, the evaluator should help the user while avoiding to give more information than necessary. The evaluator should avoid giving more information than necessary because this information may not only assist the user in handling the present problem but also convey how to handle later parts of the task. If so, the provided assistance may result in missing later usability problems. Dumas and Loring (2008) distinguish four levels of assistance that provide increasing amounts of information.

- *Breaking a repeating sequence*: Sometimes users get stuck in a sequence of actions, which they repeat several times. In these situations, a simple "What do you think is going on here?" or "Try reading the task again" is often sufficient to get them back on track. Such prompts provide minimal information about how to proceed.

- *Providing a general hint*: Users often come close to finding the right option or piece of information, but fail to notice it. In these situations, it may help to ask: "Remember how you started this task? You were getting close." If the user has not yet come close, then a useful general hint may be: "You might want to have a look at the menus you haven't opened yet."

- *Providing a specific hint*: If the previous levels of assistance are not sufficient, then the evaluator needs to turn the user's focus of attention to the relevant part of the product. Examples of such specific hints include "The information you are looking for is in the FAQ section" or "The 'wish list' is not the same as the 'shopping cart'."

- *Telling users how to do the next step*: In some situations it is preferable not to spend more time on the current step of the task because there are still several tasks left or the user is getting dispirited. Still, the assistance should as far as possible be restricted to the next step of the task, for example "Return to the previous page and click the second option."

6.4   TAKE NOTES

During a test session the evaluator has three roles. First, you must moderate the session. As a moderator, you instruct the users, make them feel at ease, remind them to think aloud, and finally thank them for their participation in the test. Second, you must do on-the-fly analysis. As an analyst, you observe the users, listen in on their thoughts, prompt them for additional information, and ask post-task questions. Third, you must take notes. As a note-taker, you log events of interest. The three roles are interconnected, for example the notes document the outcome of on-the-fly analysis. At the same time, the roles run in parallel, which makes it taxing to manage all three of them. You may consider distributing the roles among several people, especially if some of the people on the usability team are not yet experienced. In addition, equipment for recording the screen and user verbalizations (Section 5.6) reduces the need for manual note-taking. Yet, good notes are valuable even in the presence of recordings. Notes provide pointers into the recordings, thereby expediting the subsequent analysis phase.

The notes should capture what the problem is—or what hedonic experience or design possibility the evaluator has noticed. Each note should also indicate which product element it concerns (e.g., the order-confirmation page or the game-status indicator). If the sessions are recorded, then the notes should include timestamps, which make it easy to consult the associated part of the recording. If the sessions are not recorded, then the notes must also capture what happened, though necessarily in a condensed format. The description of what happened should be concrete and focus on what the user did and said, thereby providing the evaluator with a basis for subsequently analyzing the reasons why it happened. In addition, the evaluator may take temporary notes about issues that should be clarified during the post-task questions.

Kjeldskov et al. (2004) propose that the usability team runs all test sessions on the same day and meet immediately after the last session to analyze the sessions and document the identified problems. With this approach, the execution and analysis phases of the test are conducted within a single day, thereby enabling quick design iterations but also necessitating good notes. The approach resembles Krug's (2014, p. 118) recommendation that development teams should "spend one morning a month doing usability testing." However, Krug deemphasizes note-taking. The approach by Kjeldskov et al. (2004) includes a designated note-taker as well as a moderator/analyst; screen or video recordings are not employed. Because the analysis and documentation of the problems are performed immediately after the sessions, the usability team can still remember much of what happened. By walking through the note-taker's notes, they jog their memory, discuss how the users experienced the product, and agree on which problems to report. Kjeldskov et al. (2004) find that this instant-analysis approach identifies 85% of the critical problems reported in a more time-consuming usability test that identified problems by analyzing video recordings. However, the instant-analysis approach failed to identify many low-severity problems.

The designated note-taker is central to the instant-analysis approach, but it also relies on minimizing the period of time for which the usability team must remember what happened during the sessions. If the test sessions are spread over multiple days, then the need for notes or recordings increases because the evaluator can no longer rely on being able to remember what happened. Similarly, the need for notes or recordings increases if the analysis stretches over multiple days, or if test completeness is desired for problems at all levels of severity.

6.5   ASK POST-TASK QUESTIONS

The primary focus during the tasks is on the specifics of how the users experience and interact with the product. After a task has been completed, there is an opportunity for the users to take a step back and reflect on the total experience of using the product to solve the task. To facilitate comparison across sessions, the evaluator often asks all users the same predetermined post-task questions—and follow up with additional, on-the-fly questions. The questions may be asked after each task, if the answers are likely to vary across tasks in important ways. Or they may be asked after all tasks have been completed, if the intention is to obtain the users' general impression of the product.

It is often relevant to ask the users whether the task resembled how they would work with the product in a real-world situation. This question may, especially in early usability tests, reveal new information about the context of use and the user needs. It is also relevant to revisit specific parts of the task, if the evaluator has questions about how the users experienced the interaction or what caused them problems. The evaluator is particularly likely to have such questions in tests that apply classic thinking aloud and, thus, do not allow for asking these questions during the tasks. In addition, it is often relevant to ask the users whether they found the task easy or difficult and how they liked using the product. Standard instruments have been developed for gauging these aspects of the user experience. The advantage of these instruments is that they have been validated. Thus, there is good reason to believe that they measure what they purport to measure. Several of the instruments also come with reference values for assessing how well the tested product is perceived compared to other products. Tullis and Albert (2013) describe a range of standard instruments for having users rate aspects of their experience with a product. Three commonly used instruments are described in the following.

The *Task Load Index* (TLX) measures mental workload (Hart and Staveland, 1988). It consists of six items, see Table 6.4. Each item captures the users' perception of a distinct dimension of mental workload. The first three items gauge the demands posed by the task relative to the users' resources. The fourth item combines the three previous items into an aggregated rating of how effortful it was for the users to accomplish the task. The two last items give the users' assessment of their performance and process. The users rate the items on scales from 0–100. The six items can be averaged into an overall workload measure but at the expense of diagnostic power. To preserve diagnostic power, the values of all six items are often reported, thereby for example making it possible to assess whether frustration decreases over a series of usability tests.

Table 6.4: The Task Load Index (TLX), based on Hart and Staveland (1988)		
Construct	**Description**	**Response Options**
Mental demand	How much mental and perceptual activity was required (e.g., thinking, deciding, calculating, remembering, looking, and searching)?	Low (0)–High (100)
Physical demand	How much physical activity was required (e.g., pushing, pulling, turning, controlling, and activating)?	Low (0)–High (100)
Temporal demand	How much time pressure did you feel due to the rate or pace at which the tasks or task elements occurred?	Low (0)–High (100)
Effort	How hard did you have to work (mentally and physically) to accomplish your level of performance?	Low (0)–High (100)
Performance	How successful do you think you were in accomplishing the goals of the task? How satisfied were you with your performance?	Good (0)–Poor (100)
Frustration	How insecure, discouraged, irritated, stressed, and annoyed versus secure, gratified, content, relaxed, and complacent did you feel during the task?	Low (0)–High (100)

The *System Usability Scale* (SUS) yields a single number that constitutes a composite rating of the usability of the tested product (Brooke, 1996). The SUS instrument consists of ten questions that are rated on five-point scales, see Table 6.5. The ratings of the individual questions are not meaningful on their own. To calculate the SUS score, you first determine the contribution from each question. For odd-numbered questions, the contribution is the rating minus 1. For even-numbered questions, the contribution is 5 minus the rating. Then you add the ten contributions and multiply the sum by 2.5. The resulting SUS score is a number between 0 and 100.

On the basis of 206 usability tests with a total of 2324 users, Bangor et al. (2008) provide reference values for SUS scores: 25% of the usability tests yielded SUS scores (averaged across the test users) below 62, 25% in the range from 62–71, 25% in the range from 71–79, and 25% above 79. That is, a product must obtain a SUS score of at least 71 to be in the top half. Grouping the usability tests according to the type of product shows slight variation in the SUS score required to be in the top half, including 75 for graphical user interfaces, 68 for websites, and 67 for cellphone equipment.

Table 6.5: The System Usability Scale (SUS), based on Brooke (1996). All ten questions are rated on five-point scales from "Strongly disagree" (1) to "Strongly agree" (5)

#	Question
1	I think I would like to use this system frequently
2	I found the system unnecessarily complex
3	I thought the system was easy to use
4	I think that I would need the support of a technical person to be able to use this system
5	I found the various functions in this system were well integrated
6	I thought there was too much inconsistency in this system
7	I would imagine that most people would learn to use this system very quickly
8	I found this system very cumbersome to use
9	I felt very confident using the system
10	I needed to learn a lot of things before I could get going with this system

While the SUS instrument is restricted to the utilitarian aspect of product use, the *User Experience Questionnaire* (UEQ) covers both utilitarian and experiential aspects (Schrepp et al., 2017). Its 26 items tap the six constructs of attractiveness, perspicuity, efficiency, dependability, stimulation, and novelty, see Table 6.6. Attractiveness is the users' overall impression of the product. The three next constructs are pragmatic (utilitarian) qualities. The two last constructs are hedonic (experiential) qualities. To calculate the six construct scores, you first ensure that all items are coded with -3 as the negative endpoint and 3 as the positive endpoint (i.e., for the reversed items you need to invert the sign of the ratings). Then you average the ratings of the items that constitute each construct.

On the basis of data from 246 product evaluations from a total of 9905 users, Schrepp et al. (2017) provide reference values for the six UEQ constructs, see Table 6.7. For example, a product must score at least 1.17 to be in the top half for attractiveness. Because the UEQ instrument includes both pragmatic and hedonic constructs, it can be used to diagnose how a product balances these two kinds of qualities against each other. The UEQ instrument can also be used to assess whether the pragmatic qualities of a product derive from perspicuity, efficiency, or dependability and whether its hedonic qualities derive from stimulation or novelty.

Item	Item Endpoints	Reversed?
Table 6.6: The User Experience Questionnaire (UEQ), based on Schrepp et al. (2017). All 26 items are rated on seven-point scales from -3 to 3		
Attractiveness: Overall impression of the product – do users like or dislike it?		
ATT1	Annoying – Enjoyable	
ATT2	Good – Bad	Yes
ATT3	Unlikable – Pleasing	
ATT4	Unpleasant – Pleasant	
ATT5	Attractive – Unattractive	Yes
ATT6	Friendly – Unfriendly	Yes
Perspicuity: Is the product easy to understand and use?		
PER1	Not understandable – Understandable	
PER2	Easy to learn – Difficult to learn	Yes
PER3	Complicated – Easy	
PER4	Clear – Confusing	Yes
Efficiency: Can users solve their tasks without unnecessary effort?		
EFF1	Fast – Slow	Yes
EFF2	Inefficient – Efficient	
EFF3	Impractical – Practical	
EFF4	Organized – Cluttered	Yes
Dependability: Do the users feel in control of the interaction?		
DEP1	Unpredictable – Predictable	
DEP2	Obstructive – Supportive	
DEP3	Secure – Not secure	Yes
DEP4	Meets expectations – Does not meet expectations	Yes
Stimulation: Is it exciting and motivating to use the product?		
STI1	Valuable – Inferior	Yes
STI2	Boring – Exciting	
STI3	Not interesting – Interesting	
STI4	Motivating – Demotivating	Yes
Novelty: Is the product innovative and creative?		
NOV1	Creative – Dull	Yes
NOV2	Inventive – Conventional	Yes
NOV3	Usual – Leading edge	
NOV4	Conservative - Innovative	

Table 6.7: Reference values for the UEQ instrument, based on Schrepp et al. (2017)

Group	Attractiveness	Perspicuity	Efficiency	Dependability	Stimulation	Novelty
Excellent (top 10%)	1.75 – 3.00	1.90 – 3.00	1.78 – 3.00	1.65 – 3.00	1.55 – 3.00	1.40 – 3.00
Good (next 15%)	1.52 – 1.75	1.56 – 1.90	1.47 – 1.78	1.48 – 1.65	1.31 – 1.55	1.05 – 1.40
Above average (25%)	1.17 – 1.52	1.08 – 1.56	0.98 – 1.47	1.14 – 1.48	0.99 – 1.31	0.71 – 1.05
Below average (25%)	0.70 – 1.17	0.64 – 1.08	0.54 – 0.98	0.78 – 1.14	0.50 – 0.99	0.30 – 0.71
Poor (bottom 25%)	-3.00 – 0.70	-3.00 – 0.64	-3.00 – 0.54	-3.00 – 0.78	-3.00 – 0.50	-3.00 – 0.30

Tohidi et al. (2006b) has explored an alternative to asking the users questions about their experience. At the end of the test session, they ask the users to sketch their ideas for an ideal user interface on a sheet of paper. Sketching is central to ideation and design because it allows for a dialogue between the sketch and the sketcher. To use a metaphor, the sketch talks back and thereby brings out unanticipated features of the sketched design. By engaging the users in sketching, Tohidi et al. (2006b) obtain a creative kind of feedback that is very different from the feedback you obtain by having the users think aloud and answer post-task questions. Such creative feedback may be especially valuable during early usability tests.

6.6   THANK THE USER

Without test users there would be no usability tests. The users' preparedness to participate in usability tests is a prerequisite for learning about how they experience the product. The importance and value of the users' participation may already have been mentioned as an incentive during recruitment, as a welcome when the users arrived for their session, and as a motivator while solving the tasks. However, it is well worth repeating at the end of the session. It may not be obvious to the users that their, possibly unsuccessful, efforts to solve the tasks are valuable input to the usability test and design process. Rather, some users may worry that they did not perform well, in spite of your explanation that the test is about how the product performs. These users' experience of the test session can be altered by exemplifying how one of their difficulties with understanding the product has revealed possibilities for design improvements. The end of the session is also your final opportunity to answer any questions that the users may have about the test.

CHAPTER 7

Analysis: Analyzing the Data and Reporting the Findings

The analysis phase consists of turning the test data into usability findings. The primary focus will normally be on the identified usability problems but usability tests are also an opportunity to recognize the product features that work well and create good user experiences. While the usability problems should be fixed, the positive usability features should be retained. The analysis of the test sessions consists of:

- *analyzing the test data*, including considerations about what constitutes a usability problem and how many evaluators are needed (Sections 7.1–7.2);

- *rating problem severity* and, thereby, facilitating the prioritization of design resources by indicating which problems it matters the most to fix (Section 7.3);

- *devising redesign proposals* to supply the designers with inspiration for problem fixes and other design improvements (Section 7.4); and

- *reporting the test findings*, including considerations about how to ensure that the test has high impact on the continued development of the product (Section 7.5).

The analysis can partly be done in parallel with running the test sessions because the analysis of the test data starts by identifying the usability problems that surfaced in the individual sessions. Redesign proposals may also be devised in parallel with the test sessions. In contrast, problem severity cannot be rated until all sessions have been run because it depends on the number of test users who experience the problem. Table 7.1 provides a checklist for the analysis of the test sessions.

Table 7.1: Checklist – analysis
☐ Usability problems have been identified on the basis of the users' behavior and verbalizations; the evaluator has not expected that the users express all usability problems verbally
☐ If the test aims for complete coverage of the usability problems experienced by the users, then the evaluator has reviewed recordings of the test sessions
☐ The evaluator has been sensitive to the users' cultural background and, for example, attended to factors such as conversational indirectness in the analysis of the test data
☐ In important tests, at least two evaluators have independently analyzed the test data and then merged their usability findings
☐ The impact, frequency, and persistence of a problem have been taken into consideration when rating its severity
☐ Severity ratings made by a single evaluator are recognized as a weak basis for deciding which problems to fix; whenever possible, severity ratings have been made by a team of evaluators
☐ Redesign proposals have been provided as a supplement to problem descriptions, especially for the problems that do not have an obvious fix
☐ The test findings have been reported to the development team, including the location, cause, evidence, rating, and proposed solution of each problem
☐ In addition to conveying information for understanding the test findings, the evaluator has engaged in convincing the development team to prioritize the findings

7.1   ANALYZE TEST DATA

To analyze the test data, the evaluator must analyze the individual sessions and merge findings across sessions. The former serves to turn the user behavior and verbalizations into usability findings, the latter to compile the list of findings and determine their frequency. Keeping the two steps of the analysis separate produces the most comprehensive analysis. Performing both steps at the same time provides for a less time-consuming analysis. If the analysis consists of viewing recordings of the sessions, then the first step of the analysis will necessarily be to analyze each session on its own. In contrast, an analysis based exclusively on session notes allows the usability team more freedom. They may analyze the notes session by session before they compile them into a full list or they may analyze the notes in a cross-session manner from the beginning. An initial session-by-session analysis is highly recommended if the test aims for completeness or for identifying low-severity as well as high-severity problems.

Følstad et al. (2012a) report that 19% of usability practitioners make their analysis on the basis of a full review of the video-recorded sessions and 34% on the basis of a partial video review.

Studies have also investigated the relative contributions of observing the users and listening in on their thoughts. McDonald et al. (2016) find that for classic thinking aloud 51% of the problems are identified by listening in on the user verbalizations, for relaxed thinking aloud it is 68%. The remaining problems are identified by observing the users or by a combination of observing and listening. These findings indicate that thinking aloud is crucial to usability testing. However, they also indicate that the evaluator cannot rely on the users to verbalize all problems; a sizable fraction of the problems are identified, fully or partly, by observing the users.

The importance of observing the users appears to be even greater during classic than relaxed thinking aloud because the verbalizations made during classic thinking aloud are more restricted. While McDonald et al. (2016) find that the difference is not all that big (51% vs. 68%), van den Haak et al. (2004) find that only 18% of the problems identified during classic thinking aloud are identified by listening to the users' verbalizations. In their study, as much as 57% of the problems are identified by observing the users and the remaining 26% by a combination of observing and listening, thereby further emphasizing the importance of observing the users.

To turn test data into usability findings, you must be able to recognize usability problems. Virzi (1992, p. 461) defines a usability problem as "a change needed in the user interface." Such a definition says little about what the evaluator should concretely look and listen for to identify the usability problems in a product. Others have attempted to provide more concrete guidance on how to identify usability problems (e.g., Fan et al., 2019; Følstad et al., 2012a; Jacobsen et al., 1998; Stone et al., 2005). Following these studies, the evaluator who seeks to identify usability problems should analyze the test data for situations in which the following occurs.

- Users express frustration, impatience, uncertainty, or other negative emotions about the product or the fit between the product and the task. Such expressions are most evident when they are verbal, but the evaluator may also read them off the users' body language and behavior.

- Users express surprise, which indicates a mismatch between the product and the users' expectations. If the users are negatively surprised, then they likely experienced a usability problem; otherwise they likely had a positive user experience.

- Users need assistance to solve a task. Assistance should normally be held off until it is apparent that the users are stuck and why they are stuck. When this has become apparent, a usability problem has been identified.

- Users need to try several actions before they find one that brings them closer to task completion. That is, they open menus, visit webpages, choose options, and then come to realize that they are not making progress and, thus, need to backtrack.

- Without noticing it, users miss information or task steps necessary to arrive at a complete solution to a task. The users cannot raise such problems; they must be noticed by the evaluator through comparing the complete solution with the users' actions and task solution.

- The product causes mental overload by, for example, requiring that users remember complex information from early to late subtasks or continuously pace themselves to keep up with the product. A frequent indicator of increased mental load is fewer verbalizations.

- The product violates standards or conventions. Such violations make the product hard to learn because users cannot transfer experience with other products to the tested product. It also becomes harder to switch between the tested product and standard-compliant products.

- The product fails to instill trust and credibility. If so, users will be reluctant to trust the product with information as well as to trust the information provided by the product. Credibility is difficult to test in lab settings; you must be sensitive to fine changes in the user experience.

In addition to this list of criteria, the analysis may be facilitated by questions such as those for sensitizing the evaluator to the users' behavior and verbalizations (Section 6.2). However, neither criteria nor questions can quantify how much frustration, surprise, uncertainty, and so forth the users must experience before it constitutes a usability problem. To make this decision, the evaluator must analyze the specific situation and test data. For example, some product features are likely to be more central to the product than others. For the central product features, smaller difficulties qualify as usability problems. To identify small difficulties, the evaluator has more use for screen and video recordings. Some evaluators apply the additional criterion that a problem must be experienced by at least two users; that is, issues that are only experienced by a single user do not qualify as problems (Følstad et al., 2012b). However, this criterion requires a test with a fair number of users. In tests with few users, single-user issues are normally accepted as problems.

If the evaluator and the user have different cultural backgrounds, then cultural differences will complicate the analysis of the test data. For example, people with an Eastern cultural background rely more on conversational indirectness than people with a Western cultural background (Sanchez-Burks et al., 2003). Conversational indirectness is the extent to which the literal meaning of an utterance relates to what the speaker intends to communicate. Easterners tend to assume that their point has been made indirectly and with finesse. Their less confrontational way of expressing themselves may lead a Western evaluator to underestimate their dissatisfaction. For example, Vatrapu and Pérez-Quiñones (2006) find that when an Anglo-American evaluator analyzes test sessions with Indian participants then fewer usability problems are identified than when the sessions are analyzed by an Indian evaluator. Presumably, the Indian evaluator is better able to read the Indian users. In contrast, an Eastern evaluator may find Western users direct to the point of condescension. As a result, the Eastern evaluator may interpret their non-conformist expressions as evidence of poorer product usability than what they actually experienced (Clemmensen et al., 2009).

Users also experience surprise to different extents. According to Nisbett (2003), Westerners tend to perceive their world by means of logic and therefore experience surprise when things evolve in inconsistent ways. In contrast, Easterners expect less consistency and therefore experience less surprise when they are faced with changing circumstances. This difference means that the users' expressions of surprise are a more effective indicator of usability problems for Western users, who are more likely to experience and express surprise when faced with an inconsistent or standard-violating product. For Eastern users, the evaluator cannot, at least not to the same extent, rely on user-expressed surprise as a means of identifying usability problems.

To avoid culture-related misreadings of the test data, Clemmensen et al. (2009) recommend that usability tests should, if possible, be conducted and analyzed by an evaluator with a cultural background similar to that of the users. For products with a multicultural user community, there is good reason to involve evaluators with similarly diverse cultural backgrounds.

7.2   HOW MANY EVALUATORS ARE NEEDED?

Just as users differ, so do evaluators. Consequently, evaluators who analyze the same test sessions cannot be expected to report the same usability problems. On the contrary, they have been found to report substantially different sets of usability problems (Hertzum and Jacobsen, 2003). This phenomenon, known as the evaluator effect, has been documented for novice evaluators (Hornbæk and Frøkjær, 2008) as well as for evaluators with years of experience in usability testing (Hertzum et al., 2014; Kessner et al., 2001). The evaluator effect is not much smaller for the severe problems than for the full set of problems, see Figure 7.1. In short, the effect of adding another evaluator to a usability test resembles that of running another user.

Jacobsen et al. (1998) had four evaluators independently analyze four video-recorded test sessions. The average number of problems reported by one evaluator was 39.3. Thus, a usability test in which a single evaluator analyzed the four sessions would result in a list with about 39 problems. However, the modest overlap among the evaluators' lists meant that when pairs of lists were merged, the average number of problems reported across all possible groups of two evaluators was 63.2. Adding a third evaluator resulted in the identification of an average of 80.0 problems. Finally, merging the lists from all four evaluators resulted in a master list with 93 problems. Hertzum et al. (2014) made a similar study with nine rather than four evaluators and found that the identification of hitherto unreported problems continued beyond the fourth evaluator (Figure 7.1). In these two studies, a single evaluator identifies an average of 42% (Jacobsen et al., 1998) and 33% (Hertzum et al., 2014) of the total set of reported problems. That is, any individual evaluator is likely to miss the majority of the problems.

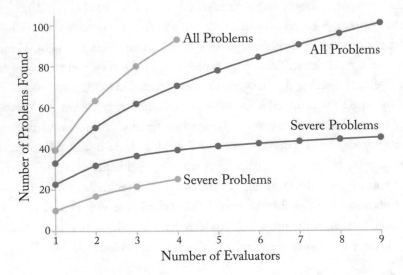

Figure 7.1: The evaluator effect. The effect of the number of evaluators on the total number of problems reported (two upper graphs) and on the subset of severe problems (two lower graphs). The two graphs with 1–4 evaluators are based on data from Jacobsen et al. (1998), the two with 1–9 evaluators on data from Hertzum et al. (2014).

Is the evaluator effect mostly caused by the reporting of different low-severity problems? To answer this question, the evaluator effect can be calculated for the subset of problems rated as severe by at least one evaluator. A single evaluator reports an average of 40% (Jacobsen et al., 1998) and 50% (Hertzum et al., 2014) of the severe problems (Figure 7.1). Some studies even find that none of the problems are reported by all evaluators; that is, there is not unanimous agreement about a single problem—severe or otherwise (Kessner et al., 2001; Molich et al., 2004).

The principal reason for the evaluator effect is that the identification of usability problems is an activity that involves judgment in a situation characterized by uncertainty (Hertzum and Jacobsen, 2003). The uncertainty is caused by vague criteria about what constitutes a problem, by the importance of local and domain knowledge to understanding the product and users, by the thin spread of such knowledge among evaluators, by dissimilar impressions of what the product seeks—or should seek—to accomplish, and by other differences among evaluators. It is impossible to eliminate these sources of uncertainty and turn usability testing into an activity that does not involve judgment. That is, the evaluator effect must be incorporated in how usability tests are conducted and test results interpreted. Any single evaluator's analysis is partial.

Due to the evaluator effect, test sessions should be analyzed by more than one evaluator, at least in important tests. It is recommended that the evaluators independently analyze the test sessions and then meet to merge their usability findings into a final problem list (Hertzum et al., 2014). A survey of 155 usability practitioners indicates that this recommendation is entering into practice: 23% of the usability practitioners report that their test sessions are independently analyzed by at least two evaluators (Følstad et al., 2012a). This way, more problems are identified and the evaluators get an opportunity to reflect on their agreements and disagreements. Følstad (2008) finds that group discussion after independent analysis also leads to a stronger focus on the more severe problems.

Alternatively, the team of evaluators may bypass independent analysis by multiple evaluators. That is, they may: (1) analyze the test sessions as a group activity; (2) collaboratively review a draft of the test report; or (3) otherwise discuss their impressions of how the users experienced the product. These alternative ways of collaborating on the analysis of the test data are more common than independent analysis by multiple evaluators (Følstad et al., 2012a). One reason for the higher incidence of these practices is their lower cost in terms of evaluator hours expended. However, they are probably less effective at identifying additional problems.

Adding more evaluators to a usability test is more costly than adding more users. It may therefore be apt to note that even though a usability test with a single evaluator is less robust, it is still worthwhile. This is especially so when multiple usability tests are conducted during the development process. Multiple tests provide repeated possibilities for identifying usability problems and reduce the consequences of missing a problem in any one test.

7.3   RATE PROBLEM SEVERITY

The analysis of the test data generates a list of the usability problems identified by the evaluator(s). The harsh reality is that it will normally not be feasible to fix all the problems on the list; prioritization is necessary. Viewed from inside a usability test, the major device for influencing this prioritization is the severity rating of the problems. However, the prioritization is also influenced by factors external to the usability test, such as how easy or difficult a problem is to fix.

The severity of a problem depends on its impact and frequency (Nielsen, 1993). Problems with high impact and high frequency are more severe than problems with either high impact or high frequency; low-impact, low-frequency problems are the least severe. Frequency is often broken into whether a problem is experienced by many or few users and whether the same user experiences the problem one or multiple times. Experiencing a problem only once means that the user learns to overcome it the first time around. In total, severity has three dimensions (Hertzum, 2006; Nielsen, 1993).

- *Impact*: how much trouble do the affected users experience?

- *Frequency*: how many users are affected by the problem?

- *Persistence*: how many times will a user be affected by the problem?

Impact is assessed on the basis of how much the affected test users are slowed down, frustrated, and otherwise bothered by the problem. Frequency is estimated by the proportion of test users who experience the problem. Persistence must be extrapolated from limited data because most test sessions are too brief to provide repeated possibilities for the user to encounter the same problem. Hertzum (2006) finds that impact and persistence are moderately correlated, impact and frequency weakly correlated, and frequency and persistence very weakly correlated. That is, each dimension expresses something that is not captured by the two other dimensions. It is therefore important that the evaluator considers all three dimensions in rating the severity of a problem.

Rubin and Chisnell (2008) recommend that the evaluator assigns each dimension a numerical rating and then sums them to get the severity rating. This recommendation serves to ensure that all three dimensions are taken into consideration. However, the more common approach is to bypass explicit ratings of the individual dimensions. The evaluator simply expresses the severity of each problem as a single rating. This approach also has the advantage of allowing for the cases in which the severity of a problem is defined by one dimension alone, such as a problem that is so obvious and so impactful that it can be a showstopper. Such a problem is high-severity even if it is experienced by only a single test user.

Table 7.2: Scheme for rating usability findings, based on Hertzum et al. (2014)	
Rating	**Description**
Critical	Critical problems cause frequent catastrophes. A catastrophe is a situation where users cannot solve a task or where the product annoys users considerably.
Major	Major problems delay or frustrate users in their use of the product but eventually allow them to continue. Major problems may cause occasional catastrophes.
Minor	Minor problems cause hesitation and uncertainty but only to the extent of briefly confusing some of the users.
Bug	The product is clearly not functioning in accordance with the design specification. Bugs include spelling errors, dead links, scripting errors, and the like.
Idea	Ideas point out missed opportunities. They are proposals from users about how to improve the user experience.
Positive	Positive issues are features and other product qualities that users appreciate. These features and qualities should be preserved.

Table 7.2 gives a scheme for rating usability findings. It includes problem severity ratings (critical, major, and minor) as well as categories for indicating bugs, ideas, and positive findings. The identification of ideas is particularly valuable during early tests of low-fidelity prototypes. It may also be important to communicate positive usability findings to the development team, for example

to verify novel design ideas or to reflect the relative weight of the negative and positive feedback obtained during the test. The later in the development process a test is conducted, the more likely it is to focus on problem identification. To rate severity, the evaluator walks through the list of usability findings. For each problem, the evaluator considers its impact, frequency, and persistence and on that basis expresses the severity of the problem by rating it as critical, major, or minor.

Severity ratings involve judgment. There are no firm rules for how frequent catastrophes must be for a problem to be critical or how much users must be delayed for a problem to be major. For example, lower thresholds will apply in safety-critical domains and for business-critical tasks. You also need to consider whether a problem could cause major difficulty for real users even though it only caused modest difficulty for the test users, or vice versa. Because severity ratings involve judgment, different evaluators cannot be assumed to assign the same rating to a problem. Hertzum et al. (2014) found that the studied evaluators unanimously agreed on their severity rating of only 20% of the problems. As much as 24% of the problems were rated as critical by one evaluator and minor by another. With so low levels of agreement, it is risky to use a single evaluator's severity ratings as the basis for decisions about which problems to fix.

The extra cost of having multiple evaluators rate problem severity will likely be small compared to both the improved robustness of the severity ratings and the cost of fixing the severe problems. When multiple evaluators rate severity, they should preferably start by independently rating problem severity, then compare their ratings, and finally reach consensus about the severity of each problem. This approach ensures that disagreements among the evaluators become visible and discussed. Alternatively, the team of evaluators may walk through the problem list together, reviewing each problem in turn and rating its severity.

In prioritizing which problems to fix, severity ratings provide important, but coarse-grained, information about how much each problem degrades the user experience. From a user-experience point of view, the most important problems to fix are the critical problems. Hertzum (2006) estimates that fixing the most severe fifth of the problems improves the user experience as much as fixing the other four fifths of the problems. While this is obviously a rough estimate, it shows that it pays to spend the majority of the redesign effort on a minority of the problems. More problems can be fixed by prioritizing those that are easy to fix, but such an approach is suboptimal unless the easy-to-fix problems are also high severity. Such a correlation cannot be assumed. That said, any problems that are both critical and easy-to-fix should be fixed first. Due to resource limitations, minor problems will likely remain unaddressed unless their solution can be bundled with the solution of more severe problems. Redesign proposals have a role in suggesting how the solution of multiple problems can be bundled in one fix.

7.4   DEVISE REDESIGN PROPOSALS

Redesign proposals supplement the reporting of identified problems by proposing improvements of the product. Most redesign proposals elaborate the description of an identified problem by proposing how the problem may be fixed. However, redesign proposals may also be unlinked to identified problems and simply express ideas about how to improve the current design of the product. Følstad et al. (2012a) find that usability practitioners are about evenly split between those who consider redesign proposals the primary outcome of a usability test and those who consider usability problems the primary outcome. This split indicates that many practitioners see redesign proposals as a more constructive way of contributing to the development process than usability problems, which focus on the shortcomings in the designers' work. By providing redesign proposals, the evaluator does not stop at criticizing but also engages in finding solutions.

Sometimes users propose redesigns, for example in response to prompts about how they experience a product feature. Open-ended tasks (Section 5.5) and user sketching (Section 6.5) are specific means of inviting redesign proposals from the users. However, most redesign proposals are devised by the evaluator during the analysis of the test data. While some redesigns will follow directly from the users' behavior and verbalizations, others will require both careful analysis to determine what caused the problem and creativity to devise a solution. A redesign proposal may address one problem or it may bundle several problems into one fix. Proposals that bundle problems are particularly valuable because they point to cost-effective uses of scarce development resources and because they indicate relations among the problems. Such relations may otherwise go unnoticed in a problem list that describes each problem individually. In devising redesign proposals, the evaluator can draw on established design patterns, on personal experience from other tests, and on guidelines specific to the domain, company, or operating system.

Compared to problem descriptions, developers find redesign proposals more useful to the further development of the tested product (Hornbæk and Frøkjær, 2005). Redesign proposals are valued for conveying ideas. That is, they are perceived as sources of inspiration and creative input rather than as ready-to-use solutions. Ideas are especially welcome when the developers are facing problems for which it is hard to think of a fix. Hence, evaluators should pay special attention to providing redesign proposals for problems that do not have an obvious solution. However, it remains doubtful whether the presence of a redesign proposal increases the likelihood that a problem is fixed (Law, 2006). Developers also tend to find redesign proposals more concrete than problem descriptions. The concreteness makes it more clear to them what the evaluator has in mind, particularly when the redesign proposals are illustrated with drawings (Hornbæk and Frøkjær, 2005).

7.5   REPORT TEST FINDINGS

The reporting of the test findings is crucial to the impact of the test. The development team is unlikely to act on the test findings unless they are reported in a manner that convinces the developers that the problems are real. If convinced, the developers need to understand the problems to be able to fix them. That is, the reporting of the test findings should make them convincing and understandable. Otherwise, it will have been wasted effort to conduct the usability test.

The test findings are typically reported in a usability test report, which is supplemented by a meeting to present and discuss the findings with the development team. Alternative formats include that the report is the deck of slides presented at the meeting or that the problems are merely documented individually in the developers' defect management system along with other revision requests and software bugs. If the usability team is separate from the development team, such as if the test is conducted by an external consultancy, then the sole means of communicating the test findings to the developers may be the test report and associated meeting. In this case, a formal report should be mandatory. If the usability and development teams overlap or have frequent interactions, then the alternative formats may be suitable.

Table 7.3: Outline of usability test report	
Section	**Description**
1. Executive summary	The main findings and recommendations of the test
2. Introduction	
2.1 Objective	Why: the objective of the test
2.2 Product	What: the tested product or prototype, including its version
3. Test plan	
3.1 Test users	Who: the number of users and their characteristics
3.2 Procedure	How: the test design and the moderation of the sessions
3.3 Test tasks	How: the list of tasks and (for specific tasks) their solutions
3.4 Post-task questions	How: any questions asked after each task or at the end of the sessions
3.5 Equipment	When and where: lab facilities, recording equipment, etc.
4. Usability findings	
4.1 List of findings	Description of each problem and positive finding, including redesign proposals
4.2 Question responses	Post-task questions, possibly benchmarked against reference values
Appendices	

Table 7.3 proposes an outline for the content of the test report. Mostly, the introduction to the report and the description of the test plan will have been written during the preparations (see Section 5.1) and can simply be copied into the report. The section about the findings must be writ-

ten during the analysis, and so must the executive summary with the conclusions and recommendations. The outline in Table 7.3 applies to formative usability tests that are conducted to inform the development team's efforts to design the product. If the test is, instead, summative and based on quantitative measurements, then ISO/IEC 25062 (2006) provides a standard reporting format, known as the Common Industry format.

Reporting the usability findings in writing provides a permanent record that can be consulted when needed, thereby facilitating a systematic approach to problem follow-up. However, test reports often do not contain all the information that developers need to fix the problems (Høegh et al., 2006). The information considered most useful by developers is the cause of the problems, followed by the interactions required to reproduce them and the location in which they occur (Yusop et al., 2016). But these three pieces of information are often insufficiently specified in test reports. One of the strengths of redesign proposals is their increased clarity compared to many problem descriptions (Hornbæk and Frøkjær, 2005). On this basis, it is recommended that the list of usability findings gives at least the following information about each finding.

- *Location*: Which product component is the finding about? Designations such as "the front page" are too vague if the front page is extensive. Annotated screenshots is a way of pinning the description of findings to specified locations.

- *Description*: What caused the problem? To identify the cause of a problem, the evaluator must get beneath its surface-level appearance and explicate its workings. At times, this will require considerable analysis.

- *Evidence*: What happened? You must describe the user behavior and verbalizations that give rise to the finding. For problems, the description of the user behavior should be sufficiently detailed to enable developers to reproduce the problem.

- *Rating*: How severe is the problem or, if the finding is not a problem, what type of finding is it? The rating is intended to support the prioritization of development resources, see Table 7.2 for categories.

- *Redesign proposal*: How can the problem be fixed? Redesign proposals are not relevant for positive findings, except if the evaluator sees a possibility for improving the product by taking further advantage of a positive finding.

Problem classification schemes have been devised to support the evaluator in identifying the cause of problems (Andre et al., 2001; Khajouei et al., 2011). If such schemes are used, then the classification of each problem should be reported. In addition to supporting developers in fixing a problem, the description of its cause also facilitates them in reflecting more broadly on their work (Vilbergsdottir et al., 2014). The developers may for example become aware of problem classes that are particularly frequent in their designs. To support such reflections further, Vilbergsdottir et al. (2014) propose extending the information recorded about each problem with the project phase in which the problem originated and the project phase in which it is fixed. These recordings may create opportunities for process improvements that remove some sources of problems from the developers' work processes.

While the test report facilitates the developers' understanding of the usability findings, video snippets from the sessions are an effective means of convincing them that the problems are real. To be able to show the developers video snippets, the users must consent to being recorded (Section 6.1) and the evaluator must mark up video segments that illuminate the main findings. If such segments have already been marked up to facilitate the data analysis, then little extra work is involved in selecting prime examples for presentation at a meeting with the development team. Watching video snippets of users who struggle to make sense of the product creates empathy with the users and a strong sense that the problems are real (Høegh et al., 2006; Yeats and Locke, 2005). Video snippets are not an alternative to a test report; they should be used to illuminate its main points. Two interrelated challenges must be considered in selecting video snippets: The snippets must be short and they must be understandable without the context of what happened before and after the snippet.

The reporting of the test findings marks the end of the usability test. However, a successfully conducted test does not in itself improve the product and user experience. To maximize test impact, the evaluator should engage in the discussion about how to prioritize the test findings vis-à-vis the other outstanding development tasks and the available resources. This discussion starts during the planning of the test and continues at the meeting where the findings are presented. It is imperative that you succeed in making the user experience an important quality parameter. Otherwise, you risk that the dominant perception of usability becomes its cost, thereby blocking efforts to fix problems and improve the user experience (Rajanen and Iivari, 2007).

CHAPTER 8

Variations and Alternatives

The preceding chapters have described and discussed the steps involved in conducting a usability test with users who think aloud in a lab-like setting. There are, however, many other methods for evaluating usability and user experience. In this final chapter, seven of these other methods are briefly described to show variations and alternatives. For the usability practitioner, knowledge of these variations and alternatives serves two purposes. It makes it easier to recognize the boundary conditions beyond which a standard usability test is no longer the better choice. And it enables the practitioner to adapt usability tests to a wider variety of practical circumstances.

8.1 REMOTE USABILITY TESTS

The target audience of many products is geographically dispersed. In these situations, it is impractical for the users to travel to the usability lab, and it is costly for the evaluator to bring the usability test to the users. To avoid that distance biases the recruitment of users, the evaluator may consider remote usability testing (Andrzejczak and Liu, 2010; Dray and Siegel, 2004; McFadden et al., 2002). In (synchronous) remote usability testing, the user and evaluator are at different physical locations and conduct the test session via video link. The evaluator instructs, prompts, observes, and listens to the users like in a standard usability test but has more restricted visual access and less control over the conditions at the users' location. In addition to reduced travel and reduced user productivity loss, remote usability tests have the advantage of allowing for culturally diverse users, who stay in a more familiar environment during the test.

Remote usability tests require additional work in planning the test. The procedure for recruiting users must reach beyond the local area and possibly include international users. For every user, the evaluator must ensure that the tested product is up and running on the user's equipment prior to the test session and that the user has access to a suitable location for the duration of the session. At the beginning of each session, the evaluator should inquire about this location. The evaluator also needs the user's help with any equipment problems, such as if the evaluator cannot see the user's screen. In addition, the evaluator should put extra effort into managing interpersonal dynamics and making the users feel at their ease. The extra effort is needed to overcome the physical separation and any differences in cultural background (Dray and Siegel, 2004). Cultural differences between evaluator and user are particularly likely in remote tests because they lend themselves to the inclusion of culturally diverse users.

Multiple studies conclude that remote usability testing is effective and leads to user behavior and usability findings similar to those of a standard usability test (Andreasen et al., 2007; McFadden et al., 2002; Sauer et al., 2019). However, some studies find that remote usability tests lead to longer task completion times (Andrzejczak and Liu, 2010) and higher mental workload (Madathil and Greenstein, 2011). While the former means that task completion times in remote and standard usability tests should probably not be compared, the latter suggests that complex test tasks will result in mental overload. Evaluators in remote usability tests must interpret the test data cautiously if the users report mental overload because it may be caused by the test situation rather than the product and tasks. When users experience mental overload, they try to compensate by changing their behavior, thereby introducing threats to the validity of the remote test. Because the evaluator in remote tests has poorer possibilities for noticing nonverbal cues and other subtle aspects of the users' behavior, Dray and Siegel (2004) recommend that remote tests are mixed with standard tests.

8.2   UNMODERATED USABILITY TESTS

Unmoderated usability tests take remote usability tests (Section 8.1) a step further by dropping the moderator. Without the presence of a moderator during the test sessions, the users perform the tasks on their own and think aloud without prompting (Hertzum et al., 2015; Tomlin, 2018). To make the sessions available for analysis, the users video-record their sessions and send them to the evaluator. As a result, the evaluator and users are involved in the test at alternating points in time: The evaluator prepares the sessions, then the users execute them, and finally the evaluator analyzes them. By withdrawing the evaluator from the execution phase, it becomes possible to run many sessions in parallel and complete this test phase quickly. This possibility of quick and low-cost scaling is the main attraction of unmoderated usability tests. To speed up tests even further, you may use one of the companies that provide unmoderated sessions as a service. These companies have a database of diverse users who have been screened for their ability to think aloud. You merely need to make the test tasks, specify the required user demographics, and wait for the session videos to be delivered for analysis.

Unmoderated usability tests are mostly used for testing web applications because they are easy to make available to the test users. In addition, the evaluator must ensure that the users have appropriate screen-recording software and instruct them about appropriate conditions for conducting the session. These instructions should include that the users must take measures to avoid distractions. In spite of the instructions, it is a weakness of unmoderated tests that the evaluator has little control over and knowledge of the conditions under which the sessions are conducted. There is no possibility to prompt for additional information during the analysis, but the videos can be reviewed for information that was missed in the first viewing. Unmoderated tests require that the users can operate the product without moderator interventions to simulate how the product responds. Thus, unmoderated tests are restricted to high-fidelity prototypes (Tomlin, 2018).

Users in moderated and unmoderated sessions make largely similar verbalizations (Hertzum et al., 2015). The main difference in verbalization content is that unmoderated users make more verbalizations of high relevance to the identification of usability problems. This finding suggests that users, at least those who volunteer for unmoderated usability tests, are capable of thinking aloud without prompting. In addition, Hertzum et al. (2014) find no difference in the total number of problems identified by evaluators who analyze moderated and unmoderated sessions. However, the evaluators who analyzed unmoderated sessions identified fewer high-severity problems. This finding suggests, contrary to Hertzum et al. (2015), that unmoderated sessions produce less convincing information about problem severity. Apart from this difference, both studies indicate that moderated and unmoderated sessions provide comparable usability information. In contrast, Liu et al. (2012) warn that an unmoderated user provides less usability information than a moderated user. Thus, it may be advisable, and doable, to run more users in an unmoderated test.

8.3   FIELD USABILITY TESTS

In field usability tests, the users exercise the prototype in vivo. That is, the test is conducted in a live situation amidst other people who go about their normal activities. While the test users still solve test tasks, they do it in a live context. The live context sets field usability tests apart from a standard usability test as well as from remote and unmoderated tests, in which the users are still in a lab-like setting away from disruptions. The live context for example makes it possible to evaluate many more aspects of the use of mobile products than in a lab, which can only replicate a subset of the settings among which mobile products travel (de Sá and Carrico, 2010). A live context also makes it possible to evaluate more aspects of cultural and organizational usability (Section 2.2). In short, the argument for conducting tests in the field is to improve their coverage and validity. The main challenges are that the test situation becomes less controllable and that equipment has to be brought along and set up in the field. These challenges threaten robustness and increase costs.

The preparations for a field usability test involve additional work to become familiar with the test site, plan how it allows for observing the test users, and possibly migrate the prototype to their equipment. If the users are in social settings during the sessions, they cannot be expected to think aloud but it may be possible for the evaluator to interject occasional questions. In addition, recordings of the sessions may be restricted to screen recordings because video recordings of the users will also capture other people from whom it is not practicably possible to obtain consent. As an alternative to thinking aloud during the sessions, the users may think aloud retrospectively cued by watching the screen recording (see Section 8.5). Or the analysis may be based entirely on the evaluator's observations and the post-task questions. In the analysis, the number of users experiencing a problem is a weaker indicator of its severity because the more uncontrolled test situation means that the users likely exercise somewhat different parts of the product.

Rosenbaum and Kantner (2007) consider field usability tests an excellent choice when the objective of the test is to collect both structured data and insights into what users really do with the product. They also recommend field usability tests when the objective is to explore which new features to add to a product. This recommendation suggests that field usability tests lend themselves more to open-ended than specific test tasks. In addition, users in field usability tests provide feedback on a broader experience than narrow product use (Racadio et al., 2012). This point is reiterated by McDonald et al. (2006), who find that only 24 (31%) of the 77 identified problems could be related to the product as such. The remaining 69% of the problems related to the context of use, including problems with the systems that were interfaced to the tested product, problems with the physical environment, and lack of documentation and training.

8.4   PAIRWISE USABILITY TESTS

In a pairwise usability test (aka co-discovery learning and constructive interaction) two users solve the tasks together. The main advantage of pairwise tests is that talking with another person about shared tasks is more natural than thinking aloud for the benefit of the evaluator. Yet, the talking between the two users provides the evaluator with information about the user experience in much the same way as thinking aloud does in a standard usability test. As an additional advantage, it takes some of the stress out of the test situation to be a pair of users working together, especially if the two users know each other beforehand. The main disadvantage of pairwise tests is that they require twice as many users as a standard usability test. That is, they are most suited for situations in which users are easy and cheap to recruit.

The preparations of a pairwise usability test become more complex if the users in a pair must know each other ahead of the test. However, with pairs of unacquainted users the test loses some of its naturalness. In addition, it should be avoided that the set-up of the test room, for example the seating of the users, inadvertently assigns the two users different roles in relation to the tested product. To counter roles in which one user takes control and the other is largely an onlooker, the evaluator should be attentive to such interpersonal dynamics and instruct both users to be active. Minimal prompting is recommended in order to allow the users to interact with the product and each other. The analysis of the test data also requires attention to interpersonal dynamics because one user's insights about how to solve a task may mask that the other user experiences problems (van den Haak et al., 2004). Also, the users may not verbalize a problem if it is apparent to them that the other user is already aware of the problem and trying to find a way around it. These interpersonal dynamics complicate the analysis of the test data.

Hackman and Biers (1992) find that users in a pairwise usability test make more verbalizations of high value to the evaluator than users in a standard usability test. Furthermore, users in a pairwise test experience their test participation as more pleasant than users in a standard usability test (Alhadreti and Mayhew, 2018a; van den Haak et al., 2004). However, these positive findings are tempered by the near absence of improved problem identification with pairwise tests. Alhadreti and Mayhew (2018a) find that pairwise tests identify more problems than a standard usability test but only because they identify more low-severity problems; van den Haak et al. (2004) find no difference in the number of problems identified with a pairwise and standard test. Without appreciable improvements in problem identification, the extra cost of needing twice as many users speaks against pairwise usability tests.

It has been argued that pairwise tests are especially suited to tests with children (Nielsen, 1993). However, for children aged 6–7, van Kesteren et al. (2003) find pairwise tests less successful than standard usability tests because the children did not collaborate very well. For children aged 13–14, Als et al. (2005) identified more problems, including more high-severity problems, with pairs of children who knew each other; there was no difference in problem identification between pairs of unacquainted children and a standard usability test.

8.5   PERFORMANCE TESTING

Thinking aloud slows users down (Fox et al., 2011; Hertzum et al., 2009). That is, thinking aloud is incompatible with the measurement of task completion times. In addition, relaxed thinking aloud is known to influence the users' behavior and performance (Ericsson and Simon, 1993; Fox et al., 2011; Hertzum et al., 2009). There is even some evidence suggesting that classic thinking aloud also influences behavior and performance (Gilhooly et al., 2010; Hertzum and Holmegaard, 2015). Consequently, thinking aloud, in particular relaxed thinking aloud, should not be used along with the measurement of task completion times and other performance measures. When such performance measures are relevant (e.g., in summative tests, see Section 3.2), then the users should not think aloud or they should do so retrospectively. Retrospective thinking aloud decouples the thinking aloud from the performance of the test tasks: The users first perform the tasks without thinking aloud and then think aloud while watching a video-recording of their task performance (Bowers and Snyder, 1990; Ramey et al., 1996; van den Haak et al., 2003; Willis and McDonald, 2016).

Retrospective thinking aloud doubles the length of the test sessions because the users must solve the tasks as well as watch the video-recording. This difference apart, retrospective thinking aloud introduces few changes to a standard usability test. During the sessions, the evaluator remains silent while the users solve the tasks, except if the users need assistance. Because the users neither think aloud nor receive prompts, their task performance is unaffected by these possible threats to validity. It is not until the users watch the video-recording that the evaluator prompts them to stimulate their retrospective verbalizations. An important side effect of having the users solve the tasks without thinking aloud is that they find performing in silence less frustrating than performing during relaxed thinking aloud (McDonald and Petrie, 2013). For classic thinking aloud, results are mixed regarding whether users perceive it as more frustrating than performing in silence (Hertzum et al., 2009; McDonald and Petrie, 2013). If the purpose of the test is to collect performance measures rather than identify usability problems, then thinking aloud may be dropped altogether.

Virzi et al. (1993) find that a performance test without retrospective thinking aloud identified 33% fewer usability problems than a standard usability test (12 vs. 18). Only two problems were unique to the performance test, ten were identified in both tests, and eight were unique to the usability test. This finding accords with the study by McDonald et al. (2016), who find that half or more of the problems identified in a usability test are identified by listening to the users' verbalizations (see Section 7.1).

If the performance test involves that the users think aloud retrospectively, then watching the video of their task performance is an effective cue for them to revisit their user experience. Bowers and Snyder (1990, p. 1273) contend that users who think aloud concurrently with solving the tasks "seem to be attending to the experimental tasks and give little thought to the comments they are making", whereas users who think aloud retrospectively "can give their full attention to the verbalization and in doing so give richer information." The two kinds of thinking aloud lead to the identification of comparable sets of usability problems (Peute et al., 2015; van den Haak et al., 2003). A possible difference is that fewer low-severity problems are identified with retrospective than concurrent thinking aloud, but about the same number of high-severity problems (Alhadreti and Mayhew, 2018b). It also makes a difference whether retrospective thinking aloud is performed after each task or not until the users have solved all tasks. The former yields more verbalizations of expectations and explanations, the latter results in lower task completion times and fewer errors made by users during the tasks (Willis and McDonald, 2016).

8.6   USABILITY SPECIFICATION

In a standard usability test, the evaluator first determines how users experience and perform with the product. Then, it is decided whether it is necessary and practicable to fix the problems identified. This approach tends to result in decreasing test impact when the development process gets into its later stages and resource limitations exert increasing pressure on decisions (Section 3.2). The evaluator can seek to counteract this pressure by establishing usability targets early in the development process. Thereby, it is first decided which usability targets the product must meet and then—when tests are later conducted—determined whether the users' experience and performance meet these preset targets. Usability targets lend themselves to inclusion in requirements specifications on par with the other requirements to the product.

Attribute	Metric	Worst Case	Target Level	Best Case	Current Level
Effectiveness of \<task\>	Number of unrecognized errors	As product Z	0	0	?
Effectiveness of \<task\>	Unassisted recovery from recognized errors	60%	70–80%	100%	?
Effectiveness of \<task\>	Number of revisits to previous screens	5–6	1–2	0	?
Efficiency of \<task\>	Task completion time (seconds), after completed training	300	90-120	45	?
Mental workload of \<task\>	Task Load Index (TLX), after completed training	60	< 40	20–30	?
Product learnability	Task completion rate for 1st and 2nd half of 20 standard tasks	Two halves equal	2nd half better	"Much" better	?
Initial assessment	System Usability Scale (SUS)	71	80	90	?
Joy of use	Questionnaire item, at the end of test session	Neutral	Somewhat positive	Highly positive	?
Preference over product Z	Questionnaire item, at the end of test session	Half prefer product Z	10% prefer product Z	None prefer Z	?

Table 8.1: Sample usability specification, based on Whiteside et al. (1988)

A usability specification should indicate what the usability targets are, how they are measured, and what the worst, target, best, and current levels are, see Table 8.1. The worst and best levels give the lowest acceptable and best attainable levels, respectively. They facilitate the decision about the target level by helping to avoid unacceptably low targets as well as unrealistically ambitious targets (Whiteside et al., 1988). In specifying the targets, you must collaborate with users to add weight to the targets and with the development team to obtain commitment to them. To reach beyond utilitarian issues and also include experiential ones, Kasinen et al. (2015) propose to seek inspiration for targets along five dimensions: (1) company or brand image; (2) empathic understanding of the use situation; (3) evidence-based knowledge of human beings; (4) possibilities and challenges of new technologies; and (5) the vision for the product. After the usability targets have been specified, their current level is measured and the process iterates until the target level is attained. The criterion for when this process ends is explicit. In a standard usability test it is not, thereby leaving the action taken in response to the test more indeterminate.

8.7   USABILITY INSPECTION

Usability inspections differ from usability tests in the fundamental way that they are analytic rather than empirical. That is, no users take part in usability inspections. The advantage of leaving out the users is that it becomes easier, quicker, and less costly to conduct evaluations. In particular, there is no lead time to recruit users and schedule test sessions. This advantage is attractive and has fostered the creation of multiple inspection methods, including heuristic evaluation and cognitive walk-through (Cheng and Mustafa, 2015; Cockton et al., 2012; Nielsen and Mack, 1994). The disadvantage of leaving out the users is the absence of first-hand information about the user experience. In place of first-hand information, the evaluator attempts to imagine or simulate how users will experience the product and which of its features that will cause problems. The different inspection methods facilitate this imagination or simulation process in different ways.

In heuristic evaluation, a group of evaluators examines the elements of the product and assesses their compliance to a small set of heuristics. The heuristics are recognized usability principles such as "speak the users' language" (Nielsen, 1993). To bolster the quality of the inspection, the evaluators should not communicate and aggregate their findings until after they have individually inspected the product. Apart from this procedural requirement, the method does not stipulate how the evaluators should apply the heuristics or organize the inspection. The resulting informality leaves much to the evaluators' skills and expertise. In contrast, cognitive walkthroughs follow a procedure that aims to produce quality results even for inexperienced evaluators. The evaluator starts by describing the typical user, defining the test tasks, and determining the correct action sequence for each task. After these preparations, the evaluator walks through the action sequences and answers four questions for each action (Wharton et al., 1994): (1) Will the user try to achieve the right effect? (2) Will the user notice that the correct action is available? (3) Will the user associate the correct action with the effect trying to be achieved? (4) If the correct action is performed, will the user see that progress is being made toward solution of the task? For each negative answer, a usability problem has been identified.

Heuristic evaluation identifies many usability problems (Hertzum et al., 2002; John and Marks, 1997). While some of these problems are severe, many are low-severity and have little impact on subsequent redesign efforts. For example, a developer was persuaded to fix only 19 (22%) of the 88 problems reported from a heuristic evaluation and rejected that 27% of the reported problems were problems at all (John and Marks, 1997). Cognitive walkthroughs tend to identify 30–50% of the problems identified with usability testing (Mahatody et al., 2010). While heuristic evaluations cover a broader range of issues (Cuomo and Bowen, 1994), cognitive walkthroughs are particularly sensitive to interface labels (e.g., links and menu items) that are unfamiliar or confusable (Blackmon et al., 2002). For both methods, a single evaluator is an insufficient basis for redesign decisions because evaluators identify substantially different sets of usability problems in heuristic evaluations (Hertzum et al., 2002; Nielsen and Landauer, 1993) as well as cognitive walkthroughs (Hertzum and Jacobsen, 1999; Huart et al., 2004). Multiple evaluators are needed for robust usability inspections.

References

Alhadreti, O. and Mayhew, P. (2018a). Are two pairs of eyes better than one? A comparison of concurrent think-aloud and co-participation methods in usability testing. *Journal of Usability Studies*, 13(4), 177–195. http://uxpajournal.org/wp-content/uploads/sites/8/pdf/JUS_Alhadreti_August2018.pdf. 81

Alhadreti, O. and Mayhew, P. (2018b). Rethinking thinking aloud: A comparison of three think-aloud protocols. In *Proceedings of the CHI2018 Conference on Human Factors in Computing Systems*. New York: ACM Press (paper 44). DOI: 10.1145/3173574.3173618. 82

Als, B.S., Jensen, J.J., and Skov, M.B. (2005). Comparison of think-aloud and constructive interaction in usability testing with children. In *Proceedings of the IDC2005 Conference on Interaction Design and Children*. New York: ACM Press (pp. 9–16). DOI: 10.1145/1109540.1109542. 81

Alves, R., Valente, P., and Nunes, N.J. (2014). The state of user experience evaluation practice. In *NordiCHI2014: Proceedings of the 8th Nordic Conference on Human-Computer Interaction*. New York: ACM Press (pp. 93–102). DOI: 10.1145/2639189.2641208. 5

Andre, T.S., Hartson, H.R., Belz, S.M., and McCreary, F.A. (2001). The user action framework: A reliable foundation for usability engineering support tools. *International Journal of Human-Computer Studies*, 54(1), 107–136. DOI: 10.1006/ijhc.2000.0441. 48, 49, 74

Andreasen, M.S., Nielsen, H.V., Schrøder, S.O., and Stage, J. (2007). What happened to remote usability testing? An empirical study of three methods. In *Proceedings of the CHI2007 Conference on Human Factors in Computing Systems*. New York: ACM Press (pp. 1405–1414). DOI: 10.1145/1240624.1240838. 78

Andrzejczak, C. and Liu, D. (2010). The effect of testing location on usability testing performance, participant stress levels, and subjective testing experience. *Journal of Systems and Software*, 83(7), 1258–1266. DOI: 10.1016/j.jss.2010.01.052. 77, 78

Arvidsson, N. (2019). *Building a Cashless Society: The Swedish Route to the Future of Cash Payments*. Cham: Springer. DOI: 10.1007/978-3-030-10689-8. 1

Bailey, R.W. (1972). Testing manual procedures in computer-based business information systems. In *Proceedings of the Human Factors Society 16th Annual Meeting*. Santa Monica, CA: HFS (pp. 395-401). 2

Bangor, A., Kortum, P.T., and Miller, J.T. (2008). An empirical evaluation of the system usability scale. *International Journal of Human-Computer Interaction*, 24(6), 574–594. DOI: 10.1080/10447310802205776. 58

Bargas-Avila, J.A. and Hornbæk, K. (2011). Old wine in new bottles or novel challenges? A critical analysis of empirical studies of user experience. In *Proceedings of the CHI2011 Conference on Human Factors in Computing Systems*. New York: ACM Press (pp. 2689–2698). DOI: 10.1145/1978942.1979336. 39

Barnum, C.M. (2011). *Usability Testing Essentials: Ready, Set... Test!* Amsterdam: Elsevier. DOI: 10.1016/B978-0-12-375092-1.00001-5. 40, 44

Bias, R.G. and Mayhew, D.J. (2005). *Cost-Justifying Usability: An Update for the Internet Age*. San Francisco, CA: Elsevier. DOI: 10.1016/B978-012095811-5/50001-8. 17

Blackmon, M.H., Polson, P.G., Kitajima, M., and Lewis, C. (2002). Cognitive walkthrough for the web. In *Proceedings of CHI2002 Conference on Human Factors in Computing Systems*. New York: ACM Press (pp. 463–470). DOI: 10.1145/503376.503459. 85

Blumer, H. (1954). What is wrong with social theory? *American Sociological Review*, 19(1), 3-10. DOI: 10.2307/2088165. 11

Boren, T. and Ramey, J. (2000). Thinking aloud: Reconciling theory and practice. *IEEE Transactions on Professional Communication*, 43(3), 261–278. DOI: 10.1109/47.867942. 52

Borsci, S., Macredie, R.D., Barnett, J., Martin, J., Kuljis, J., and Young, T. (2013). Reviewing and extending the five-user assumption: A grounded procedure for interaction evaluation. *ACM Transactions on Computer-Human Interaction*, 20(5), article 29. DOI: 10.1145/2506210. 34

Bowers, V.A. and Snyder, H.L. (1990). Concurrent versus retrospective verbal protocols for comparing window usability. In *Proceedings of the Human Factors Society 34th Annual Meeting*. Santa Monica, CA: HFS Press (pp. 1270–1274). DOI: 10.1177/154193129003401720. 81, 82

Brooke, J. (1996). SUS: A 'quick and dirty' usability scale. In P.W. Jordan, B. Thomas, B.A. Weerdmeester, and I.L. McClelland (Eds.), *Usability Evaluation in Industry*. London: Taylor and Francis (pp. 189–194). 58

Bruun, A., Gull, P., Hofmeister, L., and Stage, J. (2009). Let your users do the testing: A comparison of three remote asynchronous usability testing methods. In *Proceedings of the CHI2009 Conference on Human Factors in Computing Systems*. New York: ACM Press (pp. 1619–1628). DOI: 10.1145/1518701.1518948. 18

Burmeister, O.K. (2000). Usability testing: Revisiting informed consent procedures for testing internet sites. In J. Weckert (Ed.), *Selected Papers from the Second Australian Institute Conference on Computer Ethics*. Darlinghurst, AU: Australian Computer Society (pp. 3–9). DOI: 10.1.1.18.9392&rep=rep1&type=pdf. 45, 46

Burmeister, O.K. and Weckert, J. (2003). Applying the new software engineering code of ethics to usability engineering: A study of four cases. *Journal of Information, Communication and Ethics in Society*, 1(3), 119–132. DOI: 10.1108/14779960380000231. 45

Button, G. and Sharrock, W. (2009). *Studies of Work and the Workplace in HCI: Concepts and Techniques*. San Rafael, CA: Morgan and Claypool. DOI: 10.2200/S00177ED1V01Y-200903HCI003. 47

Buxton, M.J. (1987). Problems in the economic appraisal of new health technology: The evaluation of heart transplants in the UK. In M.F. Drummond (Ed.), *Economic Appraisal of Health Technology in the European Community*. Oxford: Oxford Medical Publications (pp. 103–118). 18

Bødker, S., and Madsen, K.H. (1998). Context: An active choice in usability work. *ACM Interactions*, 5(4), 17–25. DOI: 10.1145/278465.278469. 42

Callahan, E. (2005). Interface design and culture. In B. Cronin (Ed.), *Annual Review of Information Science and Technology*, 39. Medford, NJ: Information Today (pp. 257–310). DOI: 10.1002/aris.1440390114. 14

Catani, M.B. and Biers, D.B. (1998). Usability evaluation and prototype fidelity: Users and usability professionals. In *Proceedings of the Human Factors and Ergonomics Society 42nd Annual Meeting*. Santa Monica, CA: HFES (pp. 1331–1335), DOI: 10.1177/154193129804201901. 29

Caulton, D.A. (2001). Relaxing the homogeneity assumption in usability testing. *Behaviour and Information Technology*, 20(1), 1–7. DOI: 10.1080/01449290010020648. 37

Cheng, L.C. and Mustafa, M. (2015). A reference to usability inspection methods. In O. Hassan, S. Abidin, R. Legino, R. Anwar, and M. Kamaruzaman (Eds.), *i-CADER2014: Proceedings of the International Colloquium of Art and Design Education Research*. Singapore: Springer (pp. 407–419). DOI: 10.1007/978-981-287-332-3_43. 1, 84

Chilana, P.K., Wobbrock, J.O., and Ko, A.J. (2010). Understanding usability practices in complex domains. In *Proceedings of the CHI2010 Conference on Human Factors in Computing Systems*. New York: ACM Press (pp. 2337–2346). DOI: 10.1145/1753326.1753678. 28

Clemmensen, T., Hertzum, M., Hornbæk, K., Shi, Q., and Yammiyavar, P. (2009). Cultural cognition in usability evaluation. *Interacting with Computers*, 21(3), 212–220. DOI: 10.1016/j.intcom.2009.05.003. 2, 3, 44, 45, 67

Cockton, G. and Woolrych, A. (2002). Sale must end: Should discount methods be cleared off HCI's shelves? *ACM Interactions*, 9(5), 13–18. DOI: 10.1145/566981.566990. 19

Cockton, G., Woolrych, A., Hornbæk, K., and Frøkjær, E. (2012). Inspection-based evaluations. In J.A. Jacko (Ed.), *The Human-Computer Interaction Handbook: Fundamentals, Evolving Technologies, and Emerging Applications*. Third Edition. Boca Raton, FL: CRC Press (pp. 1279–1298). DOI: 10.1201/b11963-ch-56. 1, 84

Cordes, R.E. (2001). Task-selection bias: A case for user-defined tasks. *International Journal of Human-Computer Interaction*, 13(4), 411–419. DOI: 10.1207/S15327590IJHC1304_04. 39

Cuomo, D.L. and Bowen, C.D. (1994). Understanding usability issues addressed by three user-system interface evaluation techniques. *Interacting with Computers*, 6(1), 86–108. DOI: 10.1016/0953-5438(94)90006-X. 84

de Sá, M. and Carrico, L. (2010). Designing and evaluating mobile interaction: Challenges and trends. *Foundations and Trends in Human-Computer Interaction*, 4(3), 175–243. DOI: 10.1561/1100000025. 79

Derboven, J., de Roeck, D., Verstraete, M., Geerts, D., Schneider-Barnes, J., and Luyten, K. (2010). Comparing user interaction with low and high fidelity prototypes of tabletop surfaces. In *NordiCHI2010: Proceedings of the Sixth Nordic Conference on Human-Computer Interaction*. New York: ACM Press (pp. 148–157). DOI: 10.1145/1868914.1868935. 29

Draper, S.W. (1993). The notion of task in HCI. In *INTERCHI1993 Conference Companion on Human Factors in Computing Systems*. New York: ACM Press (pp. 207–208). DOI: 10.1145/259964.260232. 11

Dray, S. and Siegel, D. (2004). Remote possibilities? International usability testing at a distance. *ACM Interactions*, 11(2), 10–17. DOI: 10.1145/971258.971264. 77

Dumas, J.S. and Fox, J.E. (2012). Usability testing. In J.A. Jacko (Ed.), *The Human-Computer Interaction Handbook: Fundamentals, Evolving Technologies, and Emerging Applications*. Third Edition. Boca Raton, FL: CRC Press (pp. 1221–1242). 1

Dumas, J.S. and Loring, B. (2008). *Moderating Usability Tests: Principles and Practices for Interacting*. Burlington, MA: Morgan Kaufmann. DOI: 10.1016/B978-012373933-9.50005-8. 42, 53, 55

Dumas, J.S. and Redish, J.C. (1999). *A Practical Guide to Usability Testing*. Revised Edition. Exeter, UK: Intellect Books. 27, 42

Elliott, M. and Kling, R. (1997). Organizational usability of digital libraries: Case study of legal research in civil and criminal courts. *Journal of the American Society for Information Science*, 48(11), 1023–1035. DOI: 10.1002/(SICI)1097-4571(199711)48:11<1023::AID-ASI5>3.0.CO;2-Y. 13

Ericsson, K.A. and Simon, H.A. (1993). *Protocol Analysis: Verbal Reports as Data*. Revised Edition. Cambridge, MA: MIT Press. 51, 52, 81

Fan, M., Lin, J., Chung, C., and Truong, K.N. (2019). Concurrent think-aloud verbalizations and usability problems. *ACM Transactions on Computer-Human Interaction*, 26(5), article 28. DOI: 10.1145/3325281. 65

Fox, M.C., Ericsson, K.A., and Best, R. (2011). Do procedures for verbal reporting of thinking have to be reactive? A meta-analysis and recommendations for best reporting methods. *Psychological Bulletin*, 137(2), 316–344. DOI: 10.1037/a0021663. 51, 54, 81

Frandsen-Thorlacius, O., Hornbæk, K., Hertzum, M., and Clemmensen, T. (2009). Non-universal usability? A survey of how usability is understood by Chinese and Danish users. In *Proceedings of the CHI2009 Conference on Human Factors in Computing Systems*. New York: ACM Press (pp. 41–50). DOI: 10.1145/1518701.1518708. 44

Frøkjær, E., Hertzum, M., and Hornbæk, K. (2000). Measuring usability: Are effectiveness, efficiency, and satisfaction really correlated? In *Proceedings of the CHI2000 Conference on Human Factors in Computing Systems*. New York: ACM Press (pp. 345–352). DOI: 10.1145/332040.332455. 26

Følstad, A. (2008). The effect of group discussions in usability inspection: A pilot study. In *NordiCHI2008: Proceedings of the Fifth Nordic Conference on Human-Computer Interaction*. New York: ACM Press (pp. 467–470). DOI: 10.1145/1463160.1463221. 69

Følstad, A., Law, E.L.-C., and Hornbæk, K. (2012a). Analysis in practical usability evaluation: A survey study. In *Proceedings of the CHI2012 Conference on Human Factors in Computing Systems*. New York: ACM Press (pp. 2127–2136). DOI: 10.1145/2207676.2208365. 64, 65, 69, 72

Følstad, A., Law, E.L.-C., and Hornbæk, K. (2012b). Outliers in usability testing: How to treat usability problems found for only one test participant? In *NordiCHI2012: Proceedings of the Seventh Nordic Conference on Human-Computer Interaction*. New York: ACM Press (pp. 257–260). DOI: 10.1145/2399016.2399056. 66

Gentile, C., Spiller, N., and Noci, G. (2007). How to sustain the customer experience: An overview of experience components that co-create value with the customer. *European Management Journal*, 25(5), 395–410. DOI: 10.1016/j.emj.2007.08.005. 49, 50

Gilhooly, K.J., Fioratou, E., and Henretty, N. (2010). Verbalization and problem solving: Insight and spatial factors. *British Journal of Psychology*, 101(1), 81–93. DOI: 10.1348/000712609X422656. 81

Gould, J.D. (1988). How to design usable systems. In M. Helander (Ed.), *Handbook of Human-Computer Interaction*. Amsterdam: Elsevier (pp. 757–789). DOI: 10.1016/B978-0-444-70536-5.50040-3. 22

Gould, J.D., Boies, S.J., and Lewis, C. (1991). Making usable, useful productivity-enhancing computer applications. *Communications of the ACM*, 34(1), 75–85. DOI: 10.1145/99977.99993. 22

Gray, W.D. and Salzman, M.C. (1998). Damaged merchandise? A review of experiments that compare usability evaluation methods. *Human-Computer Interaction*, 13(3), 203–261. DOI: 10.1207/s15327051hci1303_2. 19

Grudin, J. (1994). Groupware and social dynamics: Eight challenges for developers. *Communications of the ACM*, 37(1), 92–105. DOI: 10.1145/175222.175230. 13, 32

Gulliksen, J., Boivie, I., and Göransson, B. (2006). Usability professionals—Current practices and future development. *Interacting with Computers*, 18(4), 568–600. DOI: 10.1016/j.intcom.2005.10.005. 5

Hackman, G.S. and Biers, D.W. (1992). Team usability testing: Are two heads better than one? In *Proceedings of the Human Factors Society 36th Annual Meeting*. Santa Monica, CA: HFS (pp. 1205–1209). DOI: 10.1177/154193129203601605. 81

Han, S.H., Yun, M.H., Kwahk, J., and Hong, S.W. (2001). Usability of consumer electronic products. *International Journal of Industrial Ergonomics*, 28(3–4), 143–151. DOI: 10.1016/S0169-8141(01)00025-7. 13

Hart, S.G. and Staveland, L.E. (1988). Development of NASA-TLX (task load index): Results of empirical and theoretical research. In P.A. Hancock and N. Meshkati (Eds.), *Human Mental Workload*. Amsterdam: North-Holland (pp. 139–183). DOI: 10.1016/S0166-4115(08)62386-9. 57, 58

Hartson, R. and Pyla, P.S. (2012). *The UX Book: Process and Guidelines for Ensuring a Quality User Experience*. Amsterdam: Morgan Kaufmann. DOI: 10.1016/B978-0-12-385241-0.00001-4. 4, 38

Hassenzahl, M. and Tractinsky, N. (2006). User experience—A research agenda. *Behaviour and Information Technology*, 25(2), 91–97. DOI: 10.1080/01449290500330331. 9

Helander, M.G. and Khalid, H.M. (2006). Affective and pleasurable design. In G. Salvendy (Ed.), *Handbook of Human Factors and Ergonomics*. Third Edition. New York: Wiley (pp. 543–572). DOI: 10.1002/0470048204.ch21. 13

Hertzum, M. (1999). User testing in industry: A case study of laboratory, workshop, and field tests. In A. Kobsa and C. Stephanidis (Eds.), *User Interfaces for All: Proceedings of the Fifth ERCIM Workshop*. Sankt Augustin, Germany: GMD (pp. 59–72). 15, 18

Hertzum, M. (2006). Problem prioritization in usability evaluation: From severity assessments toward impact on design. *International Journal of Human-Computer Interaction*, 21(2), 125–146. DOI: 10.1207/s15327590ijhc2102_2. 69, 70, 71

Hertzum, M. (2010). Images of usability. *International Journal of Human-Computer Interaction*, 26(6), 567–600. DOI: 10.1080/10447311003781300. 11, 12, 14

Hertzum, M. (2016). A usability test is not an interview. *ACM Interactions*, 23(2), 82–84. DOI: 10.1145/2875462. 53

Hertzum, M. (2018). Commentary: Usability - A sensitizing concept. *Human-Computer Interaction*, 33(2), 178–181. DOI: 10.1080/07370024.2017.1302800. 11

Hertzum, M., Borlund, P., and Kristoffersen, K.B. (2015). What do thinking-aloud participants say? A comparison of moderated and unmoderated usability sessions. *International Journal of Human-Computer Interaction*, 31(9), 557–570. DOI: 10.1080/10447318.2015.1065691. 54, 78

Hertzum, M. and Clemmensen, T. (2012). How do usability professionals construe usability? *International Journal of Human-Computer Studies*, 70(1), 26–42. DOI: 10.1016/j.ijhcs.2011.08.001. 47, 48, 49

Hertzum, M., Hansen, K.D., and Andersen, H.H.K. (2009). Scrutinising usability evaluation: Does thinking aloud affect behaviour and mental workload? *Behaviour and Information Technology*, 28(2), 165–181. DOI: 10.1080/01449290701773842. 18, 47, 51, 54, 82

Hertzum, M. and Holmegaard, K.D. (2015). Thinking aloud influences perceived time. *Human Factors*, 57(1), 101–109. DOI: 10.1177/0018720814540208. 81

Hertzum, M. and Jacobsen, N.E. (1999). The evaluator effect during first-time use of the cognitive walkthrough technique. In H.-J. Bullinger and J. Ziegler (Eds.), *Proceedings of the HCI International 1999 Conference on Human-Computer Interaction*. London: Erlbaum (Vol. 1, pp. 1063–1067). DOI: https://tinyurl.com/sb9baeb. 85

Hertzum, M. and Jacobsen, N.E. (2003). The evaluator effect: A chilling fact about usability evaluation methods. *International Journal of Human-Computer Interaction*, 15(1), 183–204. DOI: 10.1207/S15327590IJHC1501_14. 67, 68

Hertzum, M., Jacobsen, N.E., and Molich, R. (2002). Usability inspections by groups of specialists: Perceived agreement in spite of disparate observations. In *CHI2002 Extended Abstracts on Human Factors in Computing Systems*. New York: ACM Press (pp. 662–663). DOI: 10.1145/506443.506534. 84, 85

Hertzum, M. and Kristoffersen, K.B. (2018). What do usability test moderators say? 'Mm hm', 'uh-huh', and beyond. In *NordiCHI2018: Proceedings of the Tenth Nordic Conference on Human-Computer Interaction*. New York: ACM Press (pp. 364–375). DOI: 10.1145/3240167.3240181. 52

Hertzum, M., Molich, R., and Jacobsen, N.E. (2014). What you get is what you see: Revisiting the evaluator effect in usability tests. *Behaviour and Information Technology*, 33(2), 143–161. DOI: 10.1080/0144929X.2013.783114. 40, 67, 68, 70, 71

Hockenberry, B. and Blackburn, K. (2016). Get out of fines free: Recruiting student usability testers via fine waivers. *Journal of Access Services*, 13(1), 24–34. DOI: 10.1080/15367967.2016.1154466. 34

Hornbæk, K. and Frøkjær, E. (2005). Comparing usability problems and redesign proposals as input to practical systems development. In *Proceedings of the CHI2005 Conference on Human Factors in Computing Systems*. New York: ACM Press (pp. 391–400). DOI: 10.1145/1054972.1055027. 72, 74

Hornbæk, K. and Frøkjær, E. (2008). A study of the evaluator effect in usability testing. *Human-Computer Interaction*, 23(3), 251–277. DOI: 10.1080/07370020802278205. 67

Hornbæk, K. and Hertzum, M. (2017). Technology acceptance and user experience: A review of the experiential component in HCI. *ACM Transactions on Computer-Human Interaction*, 24(5), article 33. DOI: 10.1145/3127358. 13

Hornbæk, K. and Law, E.L.-C. (2007). Meta-analysis of correlations among usability measures. In *Proceedings of the CHI2007 Conference on Human Factors in Computing Systems*. New York: ACM Press (pp. 617–626). DOI: 10.1145/1240624.1240722. 26

Huart, J., Kolski, C., and Sagar, M. (2004). Evaluation of multimedia applications using inspection methods: The cognitive walkthrough case. *Interacting with Computers*, 16(2), 183–215. DOI: 10.1016/j.intcom.2003.12.005. 85

Høegh, R.T., Nielsen, C.M., Overgaard, M., Pedersen, M.B., and Stage, J. (2006). The impact of usability reports and user test observations on developers' understanding of usability data: An exploratory study. *International Journal of Human-Computer Interaction*, 21(2), 173–196. DOI: 10.1207/s15327590ijhc2102_4. 74, 75

ISO 9241. (2010). *Ergonomics of Human-System Interaction - Part 210: Human-Centred Design for Interactive Systems*. Geneva, CH: International Standard Organization. 9, 10, 11, 13, 47

ISO/IEC 25062. (2006). *Software Engineering - Software Product Quality Requirements and Evaluation (SQuaRE) - Common Industry Format (CIF) for Usability Test Reports*. Geneva, CH: International Standard Organization. 74

Jacobsen, N.E., Hertzum, M., and John, B.E. (1998). The evaluator effect in usability tests. In *CHI1998 Conference Summary on Human Factors in Computing Systems*. New York: ACM Press (pp. 255–256). DOI: 10.1145/286498.286737. 65, 67, 68

Javornik, M., Nadoh, N., and Lange, D. (2019). Data is the new oil: How data will fuel the transportation industry—The airline industry as an example. In B. Müller and G. Meyer (Eds.), *Towards User-Centric Transport in Europe: Challenges, Solutions and Collaborations*. Cham: Springer (pp. 295–308). DOI: 10.1007/978-3-319-99756-8_19. 1

John, B.E. and Marks, S.J. (1997). Tracking the effectiveness of usability evaluation methods. *Behaviour and Information Technology*, 16(4&5), 188–202. DOI: 10.1080/014492997119789. 16, 18, 84

Jordan, P.W. (1998). Human factors for pleasure in product use. *Applied Ergonomics*, 29(1), 25–33. DOI: 10.1016/S0003-6870(97)00022-7. 13

Kaasinen, E., Roto, V., Hakulinen, J., Heimonen, T., Jokinen, J.P.P., Karvonen, H., et al. (2015). Defining user experience goals to guide the design of industrial systems. *Behaviour and Information Technology*, 34(10), 976–991. DOI: 10.1080/0144929X.2015.1035335. 83

Kensing, F. and Munk-Madsen, A. (1993). PD: Structure in the toolbox. *Communications of the ACM*, 36(6), 78–85. DOI: 10.1145/153571.163278. 32

Kessner, M., Wood, J., Dillon, R.F., and West, R.L. (2001). On the reliability of usability testing. In *CHI2001 Extended Abstracts on Human Factors in Computing Systems*. New York: ACM Press (pp. 97–98). DOI: 10.1145/634067.634127. 67, 68

Khajouei, R., Peute, L.W.P., Hasman, A., and Jaspers, M.W.M. (2011). Classification and prioritization of usability problems using an augmented classification scheme. *Journal of Biomedical Informatics*, 44(6), 948–957. DOI: 10.1016/j.jbi.2011.07.002. 74

Kim, G.J. (2015). *Human-Computer Interaction: Fundamentals and Practice*. New York: Auerbach. DOI: 10.1201/b18071. 12

Kim, H.S. (2002). We talk, therefore we think? A cultural analysis of the effect of talking on thinking. *Journal of Personality and Social Psychology*, 83(4), 828–842. DOI: 10.1037/0022-3514.83.4.828. 54

Kjeldskov, J., Skov, M.B., and Stage, J. (2004). Instant data analysis: Conducting usability evaluations in a day. In *NordiCHI2004: Proceedings of the Third Nordic Conference on Human-Computer Interaction*. New York: ACM Press (pp. 233–240). DOI: 10.1145/1028014.1028050. 56

Krug, S. (2014). *Don't Make Me Think, Revisited: A Common Sense Approach to Web Usability*. San Francisco, CA: New Riders. 56

Law, E.L.-C. (2006). Evaluating the downstream utility of user tests and examining the developer effect: A case study. *International Journal of Human-Computer Interaction*, 21(2), 147–172. DOI: 10.1207/s15327590ijhc2102_3. 16

Law, E.L.-C., Roto, V., Hassenzahl, M., Vermeeren, A.P.O.S., and Kort, J. (2009). Understanding, scoping and defining user experience: A survey approach. In *Proceedings of the CHI2009 Conference on Human Factors in Computing Systems*. New York: ACM Press (pp. 719–728). DOI: 10.1145/1518701.1518813. 9

Lazar, J., Feng, J.H., and Hochheiser, H. (2010). *Research Methods in Human-Computer Interaction*. Chichester, UK: Wiley. 46

Lazar, J., Jones, A., and Shneiderman, B. (2006). Workplace user frustration with computers: An exploratory investigation of the causes and severity. *Behaviour and Information Technology*, 25(3), 239–251. DOI: 10.1080/01449290500196963. 1

Lewis, C. (1982). *Using the "Thinking-Aloud" Method in Cognitive Interface Design, RC 9265 (#40713)*. Yorktown Heights, NY: IBM Thomas Watson Research Center. 2

Lewis, J.R. (2001a). Evaluation of procedures for adjusting problem-discovery rates estimated from small samples. *International Journal of Human-Computer Interaction*, 13(4), 445–479. DOI: 10.1207/S15327590IJHC1304_06. 35

Lewis, J.R. (2001b). Introduction: Current issues in usability evaluation. *International Journal of Human-Computer Interaction*, 13(4), 343–349. DOI: 10.1207/S15327590IJHC1304_01. 16

Lewis, J.R. (2012). Usability testing. In G. Salvendy (Ed.), *Handbook of Human Factors and Ergonomics*. Fourth Edition. Hoboken, NJ: Wiley (pp. 1267–1312). DOI: 10.1002/9781118131350. ch46. 1

Lim, Y.-K., Pangam, A., Periyasami, S., and Aneja, S. (2006). Comparative analysis of high- and low-fidelity prototypes for more valid usability evaluations of mobile devices. In *NordiCHI2006: Proceedings of the Fourth Nordic Conference on Human-Computer Interaction*. New York: ACM Press (pp. 291–300). DOI: 10.1145/1182475.1182506. 29

Lindgaard, G. and Chattratichart, J. (2007). Usability testing: What have we overlooked? In *Proceedings of the CHI2007 Conference on Human Factors in Computing Systems*. New York: ACM Press.(pp. 1415–1424). DOI: 10.1145/1240624.1240839. 41

Liu, D., Bias, R.G., Lease, M., and Kuipers, R. (2012). Crowdsourcing for usability testing. *Proceedings of the American Society for Information Science and Technology*, 49(1), 1–10. DOI: 10.1002/meet.14504901100. 79

Madathil, K.C. and Greenstein, J.S. (2011). Synchronous remote usability testing - A new approach facilitated by virtual worlds. In *Proceedings of the CHI2011 Conference on Human Factors in Computing Systems*. New York: ACM Press (pp. 2225–2234). DOI: 10.1145/1978942.1979267. 78

Mahatody, T., Sagar, M., and Kolski, C. (2010). State of the art on the cognitive walkthrough method, its variants and evolutions. *International Journal of Human-Computer Interaction*, 26(8), 741–785. DOI: 10.1080/10447311003781409. 84

Marcus, A. and Gould, E.W. (2012). Globalization, localization, and cross-cultural user-interface design. In J.A. Jacko (Ed.), *The Human-Computer Interaction Handbook: Fundamentals, Evolving Technologies, and Emerging Applications*. Third Edition. Boca Raton, FL: CRC Press (pp. 341–366). DOI: 10.1201/b11963-ch-15. 14

Marshall, R., Cook, S., Mitchell, V., Summerskill, S., Haines, V., Maguire, M., Sims, R., Gyi, D., and Case, K. (2015). Design and evaluation: End users, user datasets and personas. *Applied Ergonomics*, 46, 311–317. DOI: 10.1016/j.apergo.2013.03.008. 31

McDonald, S., Edwards, H.M., and Zhao, T. (2012). Exploring think-alouds in usability testing: An international survey. *IEEE Transactions on Professional Communication*, 55(1), 2–19. DOI: 10.1109/TPC.2011.2182569. 51

McDonald, S., Monahan, K., and Cockton, G. (2006). Modified contextual design as a field evaluation method. In *NordiCHI2006: Proceedings of the Fourth Nordic Conference on Human.Computer Interaction*. New York: ACM Press (pp. 437–440). DOI: 10.1145/1182475.1182531. 80

McDonald, S. and Petrie, H. (2013). The effect of global instructions on think-aloud testing. In *Proceedings of the CHI2013 Conference on Human Factors in Computing Systems*. New York: ACM Press (pp. 2941–2944). DOI: 10.1145/2470654.2481407. 82

McDonald, S., Zhao, T., and Edwards, H.M. (2016). Look who's talking: Evaluating the utility of interventions during an interactive think-aloud. *Interacting with Computers*, 28(3), 387–403. DOI: 10.1093/iwc/iwv014. 65, 82

McFadden, E., Hager, D.R., Elie, C.J., and Blackwell, J.M. (2002). Remote usability evaluation: Overview and case studies. *International Journal of Human-Computer Interaction*, 14(3&4), 489–502. DOI: 10.1080/10447318.2002.9669131. 77, 78

McGrath, J.E. (1981). Dilemmatics: The study of research choices and dilemmas. *American Behavioral Scientist*, 25(2), 179–210. DOI: 10.1177/000276428102500205. 17

Molich, R., Ede, M.R., Kaasgaard, K., and Karyukin, B. (2004). Comparative usability evaluation. *Behaviour and Information Technology*, 23(1), 65–74. DOI: 10.1080/01449290320000173951. 68

Nielsen, J. (1993). *Usability Engineering*. Boston, MA: Academic Press. DOI: 10.1016/B978-0-08-052029-2.50012-7. 18, 38, 69

Nielsen, J. and Landauer, T.K. (1993). A mathematical model of the finding of usability problems. In *Proceedings of the INTERCHI1993 Conference on Human Factors in Computing Systems*. New York: ACM Press (pp. 206–213). DOI: DOI: 10.1145/169059.169166. 34, 81, 84, 85

Nielsen, J. and Levy, J. (1994). Measuring usability: Preferences vs. performance. *Communications of the ACM*, 37(4), 66–75. DOI: 10.1145/175276.175282. 26

Nielsen, J. and Mack, R.L. (1994). *Usability Inspection Methods*. New York: Wiley. 1, 84

Nielsen, L. (2019). *Personas—User Focused Design*. Second Edition. London: Springer. DOI: 10.1007/978-1-4471-7427-1. 31

Nisbett, R.E. (2003). *The Geography of Thought: How Asians and Westeners Think Differently - And Why*. London: Nicholas Brealey. 67

Nisbett, R.E., Peng, K., Choi, I., and Norenzayan, A. (2001). Culture and systems of thought: Holistic vs. analytic cognition. *Psychological Review*, 108(2), 291–310. DOI: 10.1037/0033-295X.108.2.291. 14

Norman, D.A. (1986). Cognitive engineering. In D.A. Norman and S.W. Draper (Eds.), *User Centered System Design: New Perspectives on Human-Computer Interaction* Hillsdale, NJ: Erlbaum (pp. 31–61). DOI: 10.1201/b15703. 48

Olmsted-Hawala, E.L., Murphy, E.D., Hawala, S., and Ashenfelter, K.T. (2010). Think-aloud protocols: A comparison of three think-aloud protocols for use in testing data-dissemination web sites for usability. In *Proceedings of the CHI2010 Conference on Human Factors in Computing Systems*. New York: ACM Press (pp. 2381–2390). DOI: 10.1145/1753326.1753685. 18

Olson, J.S. and Olson, G.M. (2014). *Working Together Apart: Collaboration over the Internet*. San Rafael, CA: Morgan and Claypool. DOI: 10.2200/S00542ED1V01Y201310HCI020. 1

Petroski, H. (1992). *The Evolution of Useful Things: How Everyday Artifacts – From Forks and Pins to Paper Clips and Zippers – Came to be as They Are*. New York: Vintage Books. 2

Peute, L.W.P., de Keizer, N.F., and Jaspers, M.W.M. (2015). The value of retrospective and concurrent think aloud in formative usability testing of a physician data query tool. *Journal of Biomedical Informatics*, 55, 1–10. DOI: 10.1016/j.jbi.2015.02.006. 82

Racadio, R., Rose, E., and Boyd, S. (2012). Designing and evaluating the mobile experience through iterative field studies. In *Proceedings of the SIGDOC2012 Conference on Design of Communication*. New York: ACM Press (pp. 191–196). DOI: 10.1145/2379057.2379095. 80

Rajanen, M. and Iivari, N. (2007). Usability cost-benefit analysis: How usability became a curse word? In *Proceedings of the INTERACT2007 Conference on Human-Computer Interaction*. London: Springer (LNCS 4663, pp. 511–524). DOI: 10.1007/978-3-540-74800-7_47. 75

Ramey, J., Rowberg, A.H., and Robinson, C. (1996). Adaptation of an ethnographic method for investigation of the task domain in diagnostic radiology. In D. Wixon and J. Ramey (Eds.), *Field Methods Casebook for Software Design*. New York: Wiley (pp. 1–15). 81

Rasmussen, R., Christensen, A.S., Fjeldsted, T., and Hertzum, M. (2011). Selecting users for participation in IT projects: Trading a representative sample for advocates and champions? *Interacting with Computers*, 23(2), 176–187. DOI: 10.1016/j.intcom.2011.02.006. 32

Redish, J. (2007). Expanding usability testing to evaluate complex systems. *Journal of Usability Studies*, 2(3), 102–111. http://uxpajournal.org/wp-content/uploads/pdf/utesting-complex-old.pdf. 28

Rogers, E.M. (2003). D*iffusion of Innovations*. Fifth Edition. New York: Free Press. 32, 33

Rosenbaum, S. and Kantner, L. (2007). Field usability testing: Method, not compromise. In *Proceedings of the IEEE International Professional Communication Conference*. Los Alamitos, CA: IEEE Press (pp. 1–7). DOI: 10.1109/IPCC.2007.4464060. 80

Rubin, J. and Chisnell, D. (2008). *Handbook of Usability Testing: How to Plan, Design, and Conduct Effective Tests*. Second Edition. Indianapolis, IN: Wiley. 27, 70

Rudd, J., Stern, K., and Isensee, S. (1996). Low vs. high-fidelity prototyping debate. *ACM Interactions*, 3(1), 76–85. DOI: 10.1145/223500.223514. 28

Sanchez-Burks, J., Lee, F., Choi, I., Nisbett, R., Zhao, S., and Koo, J. (2003). Conversing across cultures: East-West communication styles in work and nonwork contexts. *Journal of Personality and Social Psychology*, 85(2), 363–372. DOI: 10.1037/0022-3514.85.2.363. 66

Sauer, J. and Sonderegger, A. (2009). The influence of prototype fidelity and aesthetics of design in usability tests: Effects on user behaviour, subjective evaluation and emotion. *Applied Ergonomics*, 40(4), 670–677. DOI: 10.1016/j.apergo.2008.06.006. 29

Sauer, J., Sonderegger, A., Heyden, K., Biller, J., Klotz, J., and Uebelbacher, A. (2019). Extra-laboratorial usability tests: An empirical comparison of remote and classical field testing with lab testing. *Applied Ergonomics*, 74, 85–96. DOI: 10.1016/j.apergo.2018.08.011. 78

Sawyer, P., Flanders, A., and Wixon, D. (1996). Making a difference—The impact of inspections. In *Proceedings of the CHI1996 Conference on Human Factors in Computing Systems*. New York: ACM Press (pp. 376–382). DOI: 10.1145/238386.238579. 18

Schmettow, M. (2012). Sample size in usability studies. *Communications of the ACM*, 55(4), 64–70. DOI: 10.1145/2133806.2133824. 34, 36

Schrepp, M., Hinderks, A., and Thomaschewski, J. (2017). Construction of a benchmark for the user experience questionnaire (UEQ). *International Journal of Interactive Multimedia and Artificial Intelligence*, 4(4), 40–44. DOI: 10.9781/ijimai.2017.445. 59, 60, 61

Schrier, J.R. (1992). Reducing stress associated with participating in a usability test. In *Proceedings of the Human Factors Society 36th Annual Meeting*. Santa Monica, CA: HFS (pp. 1210-1214). DOI: 10.1177/154193129203601606. 41

Shackel, B. (1984). The concept of usability. In J. Bennett, D. Case, J. Sandelin, and M. Smith (Eds.), *Visual Display Terminals: Usability Issues and Health Concerns*. Englewood Cliffs, NJ: Prentice-Hall (pp. 45–87). 9

Shadish, W.R., Cook, T.D., and Campbell, D.T. (2002). *Experimental and Quasi-Experimental Designs for Generalized Causal Inference*. Boston, MA: Houghton Mifflin. 15

Sharma, A. (2013). Do we really need traditional usability lab for UX practice? In A. Chakrabarti and R.V. Prakash (Eds.), *ICoRD2013: Proceedings of the International Conference on Research into Design*. India: Springer (pp. 399–409). DOI: 10.1007/978-81-322-1050-4_324. 42

Sim, G., Cassidy, B., and Read, J.C. (2013). Understanding the fidelity effect when evaluating games with children. In *Proceedings of the IDC2013 Conference on Interaction Design and Children*. New York: ACM Press (pp. 193–200). DOI: 10.1145/2485760.2485769. 29

Skov, M.B. and Stage, J. (2012). Training software developers and designers to conduct usabiity evaluations. *Behaviour and Information Technology*, 31(4), 425–435. DOI: 10.1080/01449290903398208. 40

Snyder, C. (2003). *Paper Prototyping: The Fast and Easy Way to Design and Refine User Interfaces.* Amsterdam: Morgan Kaufmann. 30

Sommerville, I. (2016). *Software Engineering.* Tenth Edition. Boston, MA: Pearson. 4

Sova, D.H. and Nielsen, J. (2003). *234 Tips and Tricks for Recruiting Users as Participants in Usability Studies.* Fremont, CA: Nielsen Norman Group. 33

Spool, J. and Schroeder, W. (2001). Testing web sites: Five users is nowhere near enough. In *CHI2001 Conference Summary on Human Factors in Computing Systems.* New York: ACM Press (pp. 285–286). DOI: 10.1145/634067.634236. 34

Stephanidis, C., Antona, M., Savidis, A., Partarakis, N., Doulgeraki, K., and Leonides, A. (2012). Design for all: Computer-assisted design of user interface adaptation. In G. Salvendy (Ed.), *Handbook of Human Factors and Ergonomics.* Fourth Edition. Hoboken, NJ: Wiley (pp. 1484–1507). DOI: 10.1002/9781118131350.ch54. 11

Stone, D., Jarrett, C., Woodroffe, M., and Minocha, S. (2005). *User Interface Design and Evaluation.* San Francisco, CA: Morgan Kaufmann. 65

Tarkkanen, K. and Harkke, V. (2019). Scope for usability tests in IS development. In *ECIS2019: Proceedings of the European Conference on Information Systems.* Atlanta, GA: AIS (paper 177). https://aisel.aisnet.org/ecis2019_rp/177. 39

Thomas, J.C. and Kellogg, W.A. (1989). Minimizing ecological gaps in interface design. *IEEE Software*, 6(1), 78–86. DOI: 10.1109/52.16905. 16

Thorell, L.G. and Smith, W.J. (1990). *Using Computer Color Effectively: An Illustrated Reference.* Englewood Cliffs, NJ: Prentice Hall. 14

Thulin, E. and Vilhelmson, B. (2019). More at home, more alone? Youth, digital media and the everyday use of time and space. *Geoforum*, 100, 41–50. DOI: 10.1016/j.geoforum.2019.02.010. 1

Tohidi, M., Buxton, W., Baecker, R., and Sellen, A. (2006a). Getting the right design and the design right: Testing many is better than one. In *Proceedings of the CHI2006 Conference on Human Factors in Computing Systems.* New York: ACM Press (pp. 1243–1252). DOI: 10.1145/1124772.1124960. 29, 30

Tohidi, M., Buxton, W., Baecker, R., and Sellen, A. (2006b). User sketches: A quick, inexpensive, and effective way to elicit more reflective user feedback. In *NordiCHI2006: Proceedings of the Fourth Nordic Conference on Human–Computer Interaction.* New York: ACM Press (pp. 105–114) DOI: 10.1145/1182475.1182487. 61

Tomlin, W.C. (2018). *UX Optimization: Combining Behavioral UX and Usability Testing Data to Optimize Websites.* Berkeley, CA: Apress. DOI: 10.1007/978-1-4842-3867-7. 78

Tractinsky, N. (2018). The usability construct: A dead end? *Human–Computer Interaction,* 33(2), 131–177. DOI: 10.1080/07370024.2017.1298038. 10, 11

Tullis, T. and Albert, B. (2013). *Measuring the User Experience: Collecting, Analyzing, and Presenting Usability Metrics.* Second Edition. Burlington, MA: Morgan Kaufmann. DOI: 10.1016/B978-0-12-415781-1.00011-X. 57

Turner, C.W., Lewis, J.R., and Nielsen, J. (2006). Determining usability test sample size. In W. Karkowski (Ed.), *International Encyclopedia of Ergonomics and Human Factors.* Second Edition. Boca Raton, FL: CRC Press (pp. 3084–3088). 36

van den Haak, M.J., de Jong, M.D.T., and Schellens, P.J. (2003). Retrospective vs. concurrent think-aloud protocols: Testing the usability of an online library catalogue. *Behaviour and Information Technology,* 22(5), 339–351. DOI: 10.1080/0044929031000. 81, 82

van den Haak, M.J., de Jong, M.D.T., and Schellens, P.J. (2004). Employing think-aloud protocols and constructive interaction to test the usability of online library catalogues: A methodological comparison. *Interacting with Computers,* 16(6), 1153–1170. DOI: 10.1016/j.intcom.2004.07.007. 65, 80, 81

van Kesteren, I.E.H., Bekker, M.M., Vermeeren, A.P.O.S., and Lloyd, P.A. (2003). Assessing usability evaluation methods on their effectiveness to elicit verbal comments from children subjects. In *Proceedings of the IDC2003 Conference on Interaction Design and Children.* New York: ACM Press (pp. 41–49). DOI: 10.1145/953536.953544. 81

Vatrapu, R. and Pérez-Quiñones, M.A. (2006). Culture and usability evaluation: The effects of culture in structured interviews. *Journal of Usability Studies,* 1(4), 156–170. http://uxpa-journal.org/wp-content/uploads/sites/8/pdf/JUS_Vatrapu_Aug2006.pdf. 66

Vilbergsdottir, S.G., Hvannberg, E.T., and Law, E.L.-C. (2014). Assessing the reliability, validity and acceptance of a classification scheme of usability problems (CUP). *Journal of Systems and Software,* 87, 18–37. DOI: 10.1016/j.jss.2013.08.014. 74, 75

Virzi, R.A. (1992). Refining the test phase of usability evaluations: How many subjects is enough? *Human Factors,* 34(4), 457–468. DOI: 10.1177/001872089203400407. 34, 35, 65

Virzi, R.A., Sokolov, J.L., and Karis, D. (1996). Usability problem identification using both low- and high-fidelity prototypes. In *Proceedings of the CHI1996 Conference on Human Factors in*

Computing Systems. New York: ACM Press (pp. 236–243). DOI: 10.1145/238386.238516. 29

Virzi, R.A., Sorce, J.F., and Herbert, L.B. (1993). A comparison of three usability evaluation methods: Heuristic, think-aloud, and performance testing. In *Proceedings of the Human Factors and Ergonomics Society 37th Annual Meeting.* Santa Monica, CA: HFES (pp. 309–313). DOI: 10.1177/154193129303700412. 82

von Hippel, E. (1986). Lead users: A source of novel product concepts. *Management Science,* 32(7), 791–805. DOI: 10.1287/mnsc.32.7.791. 33

Vredenburg, K., Mao, J.-Y., Smith, P.W., and Carey, T. (2002). A survey of user-centered design practice. In *Proceedings of the CHI2002 Conference on Human Factors in Computing Systems.* New York: ACM Press (pp. 471–478). DOI: 10.1145/503376.503460. 5

Wand, J.N., Shotts, K.W., Sekhon, J.S., Mebane, W.R., Herron, M.C., and Brady, H.E. (2001). The butterfly did it: The aberrant vote for Buchanan in Palm Beach. *American Political Science Review,* 95(4), 793–810. DOI: 10.1017/S000305540040002X. 1, 2

Weijer, C. (2000). The ethical analysis of risk. *Journal of Law, Medicine and Ethics,* 28(4), 344–361. DOI: 10.1111/j.1748-720X.2000.tb00686.x. 45

Wharton, C., Rieman, J., Lewis, C., and Polson, P. (1994). The cognitive walkthrough method: A practitioner's guide. In J. Nielsen and R.L. Mack (Eds.), *Usability Inspection Methods.* New York: Wiley (pp. 105–140). 84

Whiteside, J., Bennett, J., and Holtzblatt, K. (1988). Usability engineering: Our experience and evolution. In M. Helander (Ed.), *Handbook of Human-Computer Interaction.* Amsterdam: Elsevier (pp. 791–817). DOI: 10.1016/B978-0-444-70536-5.50041-5. 18, 83

Willis, L.M., and McDonald, S. (2016). Retrospective protocols in usability testing: A comparison of post-session RTA versus post-task RTA reports. *Behaviour and Information Technology,* 35(8), 628–643. DOI: 10.1080/0144929X.2016.1175506. 81, 82

Wilson, C. (2007). Ethical dilemmas redux. *ACM Interactions,* 14(4), 50–51. DOI: 10.1145/1273961.1273990. 42, 46

Wixon, D. (2003). Evaluating usability methods: Why the current literature fails the practitioner. *ACM Interactions,* 10(4), 28–34. DOI: 10.1145/838830.838870. 18, 37

Yeats, D. and Locke, C. (2005). The role of the highlights video in usability testing: Rhetorical and generic expectations. *Technical Communication,* 52(2), 156–162. 75

Yusop, N.S.M., Grundy, J., and Vasa, R. (2016). Reporting usability defects - Do reporters report what software developers need? In *EASE2016: Proceedings of the 20th International Con-*

ference on Evaluation and Assessment in Software Engineering. New York: ACM Press (paper 38). DOI: 10.1145/2915970.2915995. 74

Zhao, T. and McDonald, S. (2010). Keep talking: An analysis of participant utterances gathered using two concurrent think-aloud methods. In *NordiCHI2010: Proceedings of the Sixth Nordic Conference on Human-Computer Interaction.* New York: ACM Press (pp. 581–590). DOI: 10.1145/1868914.1868979. 53, 54

Author Biography

Morten Hertzum is a Professor of Information Science in the Department of Communication at the University of Copenhagen, Denmark. He has a Ph.D. in Computer Science and has previously held positions at Roskilde University, University of Strathclyde, Risø National Laboratory, and University of Limerick. Hertzum has published extensively about usability and user experience, especially about methods for their evaluation. He is also co-editor of the book *Situated Design Methods* (MIT Press, 2014). His research interests include human-computer interaction, computer supported cooperative work, information seeking, and healthcare informatics.

Printed in the United States
by Baker & Taylor Publisher Services